Housekeeper Desired

MARTHA F. SWAIN

Copyright © 2017 Martha F. Swain

All rights reserved.

ISBN:1547068051

ISBN-13:9781547068050

DEDICATION

The publishing of this book is dedicated to the author who long ago wrote this novel but never published. I hope that seeing your published work, available to the world, brings you happiness and a sense of fulfillment. I, the author's son, having completely underestimated the effort of transcribing the paper manuscript relative to my deadline, hereby take all responsibility for typographical and grammatical errors.

CONTENTS

	Acknowledgments	i
1	Chapter One	1
2	Chapter Two	16
3	Chapter Three	31
4	Chapter Four	42
5	Chapter Five	51
6	Chapter Six	63
7	Chapter Seven	79
8	Chapter Eight	95
9	Chapter Nine	111
10	Chapter Ten	125
11	Chapter Eleven	141
12	Chapter Twelve	160
13	Chapter Thirteen	176
14	Chapter Fourteen	196
	About the Author	212

ACKNOWLEDGMENTS

I am writing this, not as the author, but as a proud son who is publishing this work as a birthday gift. I would to thank my brother Mark, without whose surreptitious obtaining of the hand-typed manuscript, this effort would not be possible. I would also like to thank my daughter (and author's granddaughter) Carly for creating the book's cover. And lastly, the author herself for creating this work and being the parent and teacher that anyone would be lucky to have.

1 CHAPTER ONE

"Down, two, three and left, two, three and right, two, three." Molly led the ladies, varying in age, shape and physical condition, through the routine she knew so well. Though air-conditioned, the exercise salon was small and the more than twenty perspiring women created more heat than the hard working machine could cope with on such a hot, humid day. A group this large also challenged the capacity of the room as each aspirer to a more perfect figure required room to stretch out on the floor and move freely in either direction. This was a group session and Molly noted with relief that according to the large wall clock, the required twenty minutes of non-stop exercise was almost up.

Her smile was pasted on and her voice was a recording of the hundreds of times she had done this same routine. Often she threw in some variations to break the monotony for herself and the clients and occasionally directed a humorous remark at a regular that she knew would take it in fun, as it was meant, but not today. Her body was moving, by remote control, gracefully through ten repetitions of each exercise, while her mind was on this morning's confrontation with Isadora.

Molly was an unassuming girl who usually took whatever life dealt her in stride. She was prompt, worked hard and had maintained the always cheerful attitude that was required of a good technician. She did not expect compliments for doing her job and, indeed, had no idea that there wasn't a female in the room that didn't admire, envy, or even resent the long, slender limbs and body which were softened by gently curving hips and the high proud breasts that maintained their shape even under the tight black leotard. But she had worked here for a year now with no increase in pay and the minimum wage was just not enough, even with her second job, to make ends meet. So this morning she had cornered the illusive Isadora and asked for a raise.

Isadora LaSalle owned this and several other salons in surrounding communities. No one dared guess her age and the mask of make-up, still trim body, and carefully chosen designer clothes would probably keep her age a secret for years to come. Her face, beneath the lacquered platinum hair, was always impassive. Only the almost black eyes were allowed to display emotion, as if the mask might crack or lines be etched if she smiled or frowned. Despite her glamourous image, she was a business woman and had started her enterprise from the ground up. She had gradually expanded in territory and services which had been eagerly paid for by hundreds of women who wanted to be made over in her image. She usually breezed into the salon about once a week, unannounced, and almost always at an inopportune time, to check the books and confer with Allison, the technician-manager.

This morning Molly had seen her platinum Cadillac parked in the lot when she arrived at work and headed straight for the office before she could get away.

Isadora was pleasant. She was always pleasant even when she was being critical or downright insulting. She was so appreciative of the excellent image that Molly maintained in the salon, both her physical attractiveness and her rapport with the members of the staff and the clients. She truly would like to reward her financially but with the added staff and the purchase of the weight machines, it was out of the question. She would get back to her in a few months, she was assured, and she would certainly not even consider giving anyone else an increase until Molly had one.

Molly went to the dressing room feeling like she had heard a well-rehearsed and often repeated speech. Now what? She couldn't risk quitting unless she had another job lined up and she had little time to look, working three nights a week and both days of the weekend in a restaurant down the street from the salon. When she thought about how she had dropped out of the university to work for a year or so, she could have cried. But she didn't. Too many tears had been shed already in the one year that had grown to two. Now it seemed that her hopes of ever finishing were down the drain like yesterday's dish water.

She could have done it if she'd been on her own, but not with her family depending on her for help. She had been tempted many times to leave home and use the fruits of her long hours of hard work to finish school and pursue the careers she so badly wanted. But when she looked at the tired eyes of her mother and the innocent ones of her brother and sister, she know she could never just walk out and leave them.

Her father was a different story. When he came home intoxicated on liquor paid for with money that should be sending her to school or spent on bills or repairing the house, she became so frustrated that she would leave the house and walk for hours until she thought he would be asleep or gone again. Or she would retreat to the grove of pines she had discovered, and dream of better days, both past and future.

It hadn't always been this way. When Dad had been working he was a good father and the only time he drank was a cold beer after work and an occasional night out with some friends. Then, in the spring of her freshman year at college, he had been laid off. A recession in the machine tool trade left hundreds in the area unemployed and after months of trying to find a job that would pay anywhere near his old salary, he seemed to have stopped trying. The after work beer became two six packs a day and the trips to the bar were frequent, with or without buddies to accompany him.

Her mother had picked up several house cleaning jobs, all part time. She had a pretty full schedule during most of the year, but now that summer was here, there were many cancellations because of vacations. Mike had a morning and afternoon paper route and mowed a few lawns. He was only twelve and it was hard for him to find anything that paid well. Her sister, Maria, had turned sixteen this spring and had landed a job in a department store. It was hard for Molly to resent the two of them spending their money on the clothes, records and other things so important to a teenager. After all, it wasn't that long ago that she had been one herself.

As important as the money she contributed to the household expenses, was the stability that she provided. Her mother was not a confident or secure person about making decisions and Mike and Maria brought all the little problems and secrets they needed to share with someone to their older sister.

"Nine, ten!" With a final forward stretch, Molly's artificial smile widened a bit, and became almost genuine, as she said, "That's all ladies. You did a great job today!"

There was a scramble of multi-colored tights and leotards as the bodies, ranging from scarecrow to obese, scrambled to their feet and headed for the dressing room. A few die-hards climbed on exercise bikes or went to the weight machines. Molly exchanged pleasantries with Mrs. Clark, who preferred to be called Effie. She was a plump, jolly, middle-aged lady that was one of Molly's favorites. She and her husband had just returned from a trip to Europe and she was eager to share her experiences with someone. But they were interrupted by Myra, another technician and Molly's best friend.

"Molly, telephone," she called. Molly excused herself and took the receiver that Myra was extending from the cubicle where she was advising a lady about diet.

"You'll have to take it out here," she said ruefully. "Her majesty is still in the office."

"That's okay. I don't expect it's important." Then into the phone, "Hello?"

"Is this Molly Stark?", the voice was male, no-nonsense, almost curt.

"Yes, this is Molly Stark."

"I was given your name and this number to call by Alice Ford. I assume you know her?"

"Oh yes, Mrs. Ford is a regular here."

"Here?"

"I thought you knew. This is an exercise salon. Mrs. Ford is a member and comes in regularly."

"I see. Well, since this small community boasts no employment agency, it seems I am forced to try to find some household help by asking around. Mrs. Ford is my neighbor and, when I approached her about finding someone to be a housekeeper, she said she believed your mother did that sort of thing and might be available. There seems to be no listing in the directory for a Stark, so I am calling you for more information."

"It's an unlisted number. Yes, my mother does do some housecleaning. She has several part-time jobs. Perhaps she could help you out Mr. ...", her voice trailed off as she realized he had not given his name.

"I am in search of a full time, live-in housekeeper. I presently have a once a week cleaning woman and would continue to employ her. I need someone to cook and serve meals, arrange for entertaining, answer the phone and tend to a number of errands. I am willing to offer the right person a very generous salary."

Molly thought to herself that it sounded like he needed a wife, but into the phone she said, "I don't believe my mother could consider living away from home as she is needed to look after my father and younger brother and sister."

"I am in need of someone right away and haven't had any success. Do you think she might consider it for - and the figure he named was more than her two jobs were paying her – with one full and two half days a week off?"

Molly didn't give herself time to think twice. "My mother just wouldn't consent to being away from home so much, no matter how good the salary, but I would be very interested in such a position myself." Her pulse quickened as she thought about how satisfying it would be to tell Isadora she was leaving for a better paying job. And even more exciting was the thought of being able to move out of the house, away from the drunken raving and lack of privacy to be found in the small story and a half frame building she called home. And she would still be able to help financially, even more than now.

There was a long moment of silence on the other end of the connection and then he said, "I would gather that you are very young to handle such a position, Miss Stark, and inexperienced."

"I'm nearly twenty-one." Why did she say that? It made her sound childish and defensive. Then she continued, "I have one year of college, which I had to leave due to helping my family financially. I have been working here for a year and I also work as a waitress nights and weekends. I have always done part of the cooking at home, as well as other chores. I'm sure I could handle the job, if given a chance. It would be a great help to me in saving money so I can go back to college in a year or two."

His voice did not sound enthused when he said, "This is against my better judgement, Miss Stark, but since I am really in a corner right now and since you sound very sincere, I will interview you and then give you an answer."

"Thank you. I really appreciate the opportunity. When would you want me to come for the interview?"

"Right now would be best for me, but I'm sure that's not convenient for you."

How she wished she could march out of here right now and never come back, but this job was far from being a sure thing and she couldn't afford to burn her bridges just yet. "I'm working here until five and at my other job until eleven."

"When is your dinner hour?"

"I don't have one. I have a half hour to change into my uniform and walk to the restaurant which is just down the street. I just grab a quick bite before I start working."

"You don't drive? I'm afraid that would be required in this job."

"Oh yes, I do drive! But I don't have my own car and Mother needs the family car for her jobs during the day, " Oh, dear, she hoped that not having a car wasn't going to ruin her chance at least for an interview for the job.

"I will give you my number and you can call me in the morning. I'll know my schedule better then, and I'm sure we can arrange a time that will be mutually satisfactory."

She wrote the number that he gave on the corner of a diet chart that was laying on the desk, tore it off and tucked it inside the neckline of her leotard.

For the rest of the day she went through the motions of instructing new members in the use of weights and led groups in both exercises and aerobics. But her thoughts were on what one job instead of two would mean to her in terms of rest and relaxation and what more income could do for her family and her chances of going back to school. She would prepare herself very carefully for this interview, making her appearance and demeanor as mature and confident as possible.

At five o'clock she went into the dressing room and stripped off her leotard and tights. She washed as best she could from the small lavatory, wishing, as she did every Monday, Wednesday and Friday, that the facilities here included a shower. Then into her waitress uniform, hair quickly tied back with a black ribbon, a dash of lipstick and she was out the door headed for her other job. She consulted her watch. Five minutes to walk and ten minutes to grab a bite to eat.

The late afternoon sun was still hot and the humidity oppressive as she headed across the paved parking lot. This was Friday and she could look forward to a busy night at the restaurant. Lost in thought, she jumped when a car horn sounded very close to her. She looked up impatiently at the shiny gray, expensive looking car. The windows were tinted glass but it was very close and she could see that the tall figure behind the wheel was definitely masculine. She case a scathing glance in his direction, turned and started purposefully on her way again. The horn let out another blast. Really! She had enough on her mind right now without being harassed by some would-be wolf. The she heard her name being called.

"Miss Stark? Are you Molly Stark?"

She halted and reluctantly turned her attention back to the luxurious automobile and its persistent driver. The door swung open and a tall, very tall, figure emerged. Somehow, as she looked up at his almost overwhelming presence, she felt as she had when she was very young and had found herself in close proximity to a uniformed policeman.

Her voice sounded quite tentative to her own ears as she said, "Yes, I'm Molly Stark."

"We talked on the phone regarding employment today."

"Oh , yes." Now I've really blown it, she thought, with my behavior, my appearance in this ugly uniform and I can't think of one intelligent thing to say.

"I don't think you gave your name, Mr. –" and she waited expectantly for him to bill in the blank.

"No I didn't, did I? Please get in the care. I know you are in a hurry to get to your other job. Ill drive you there in air-conditioned comfort and interview you at the same time."

It did seem too bad to be put at such a disadvantage when the prospects of the job seemed quite remote, even under the best of circumstances, but there was no graceful way out and she walked silently ahead of him to the passenger side of the car and slid in on the smooth, cool leather seat. He got in himself, put the car in gear and, finding a break in traffic, eased the luxurious machine over the low curb and out onto the street.

"Where do you work?"

"At Musky's in the mall."

"I'm not familiar with the restaurant, but I know the mall."

No, he wouldn't be familiar with Musky's, she thought almost resentfully. By the looks of his car and clothes, he was used to much more elegant dining than Musky's provided.

He continued. "Now, Molly Stark, almost twenty-one, what are your qualifications for being employed by me?"

She stared straight ahead and recited, almost like a verse at Sunday school, "I have never held a position such as you describe, but I am a competent cook and can handle routine housework and laundry. I'm used to working long hours and both my jobs require meeting and coping with many kinds of people."

"You said you had a year in college. What did you study?"

"Mostly basics... English, math, psychology and art. I hadn't decided on a major yet."

"Secretarial skills?"

"You didn't mention that when we talked on the phone. I thought you wanted a housekeeper."

"I do, but the salary is high because I may require a number of other services on occasion."

"I type competently, but not with secretarial speed, and I don't know short hand or any other secretary type things."

They had pulled up in front of Musky's and Molly, feeling she had bombed about as badly as one could at the job interview, met his gray-blue eyes with her gold flecked brown ones. "I'm sorry to have wasted your time, Mr. – I still don't know your name." He still did not supply it, so she continued. "I appreciate the opportunity and I hope you find someone suitable soon."

She turned and reached for the door handle. A firm hand caught her arm and kept her from getting out of the car.

"I always make my own decisions when it comes to hiring and firing, Miss Stark. And I've not made one yet." A muscle in his jaw twitched slightly and his had gripped the slender arm with increased pressure. "I have some things to do and some thinking. You'll be hearing from me within a short time."

"Please, I must go in now or I'll be late." He released her arm and she slid quickly out of the car and scooted into the restaurant.

She barely made it through the door on time, grabbed an apron and her order pad and was thrust into the mayhem that was Friday night at Musky's. There was no break in business and she managed only a few quick gulps of milk to help allay the feeling of faintness in her empty stomach.

By the time she had a minute to glance at the clock, it was

nearly closing time. Fifteen more minutes and she could go home and shower and sleep, with luck for two or three peaceful hours, before her father came staggering in and woke the household and half the neighborhood with his drunken loudness.

She was attacking the disgusting mess left behind by a large group of high-spirited teenagers, when she heard her name spoken in that unmistakable voice. Sponge in hand, she turned and raised her weary eyes the necessary distance to meet his.

"I really wish I knew what to call you," she said.

His mouth twitched just a bit, but he didn't quite smile. "How about Boss," he drawled.

"Oh, I don't think –" Then it registered with her what he was saying. "You mean I have the job?" she asked in disbelief.

"I decided to give you a chance, Miss Stark. I don't have a lot of time to look for what I had in mind, and which may not even exist, for all I know."

"Thank you. I'll try very hard to do a good job. When would you want me to start?"

"Tomorrow."

"I really should give some notice here and I suppose at the salon, though I think Isadora won't be too surprised that I'm leaving."

"Is that rotund fellow giving us the evil eye your boss?" he asked.

"Yes, that's Mr. Gresham. I'm supposed to work here tomorrow and Sunday. He'll be furious if I quit now."

"I'm sure he doesn't want to lose a hard worker, but I'm also sure he has a list of teenagers waiting for the job. Take a deep breath and get ready to face him. He's headed this way."

Mr. Gresham approached them with his waddling shuffle, face flushed with heat, exertion and displeasure. "Molly, you know socializing is not allowed on the job," he wheezed.

Molly opened her mouth to reply, but her nameless new employer spoke before any words could come out. "Surely Miss Stark won't break you if she chats for a couple minutes just before closing time."

The chubby Gresham was disconcerted by this intervention and his florid face became almost purple. "Five minutes here and there all add up," he whined. "Rules are rules."

"Of course I realize that, being a businessman myself. But Miss Stark is, as of now, my employee instead of yours, and so will no longer be complying with your rules. I'm sure you have her address and will promptly forward any pay she has coming."

Gresham's loose jaw dropped open, multiplying his several chins by two. Molly almost felt sorry for him as he was so obviously no match for the tall, calm man at her side. Almost, but not quite. He had not been an easy or appreciative employer and, taking confidence from the support of her new boss, she whisked off her apron, laid it across his floundering arm and swept off to the kitchen to collect her belongings.

She called a cheerful goodnight to the other employees, none of whom had witnessed the scene, and joined her champion at the door. Even when tired, she carried herself tall and straight and she lifted he chin just a trifle higher as she felt his appraising eyes following her progress across the room. He held the door open for her and she said softly, "Thanks, Boss," as she stepped ahead of him out into the balmy night.

Holding her arm lightly, he guided her to the waiting car. When they were both installed in the comfort of the plush vehicle, he asked, "Did you eat?"

"I didn't have time, but I'm fine."

"Nonsense. I don't want any employees of mine malnourished. Besides, I'm sure it's my fault that you didn't have time to eat, I could use a bite myself. I've been rather busy since I saw you earlier."

Molly leaned back in the ultra-comfortable seat and looking up, saw an orange moon glowing mellowly through the opening in the car roof. "How lovely," she said with a sigh.

"How lovely, indeed," he observed but he hadn't even glanced at the moon.

They drove for a few minutes in silence and Molly wished she could float on this lovely cloud forever. Her exhausting day was beginning to overtake her and she closed her eyes and let the soft, warm air caress her face as the rolled smoothly through the almost deserted streets. All too soon, the sensation of floating stopped and she forced her heavy lids open. They had pulled into a drive-in restaurant and she blinked as the lights assaulted her unprepared eyes.

"What would you like to eat?" he inquired.

"Just some coffee would be fine."

He turned to the car-hop who had just come up to the car window and ordered cheeseburgers and coffee for two. Then he leaned aback against the seat as if he, too, had had a long day.

"Thank you again, for everything," she ventured and was suddenly shy, as she realized how isolated from the rest of the world they seemed to be right now.

His eyes lazily sought hers in the dimness of the car.

"Don't thank me yet, Molly Stark," he said. "I expect you will earn every cent I pay you and then some."

"I expect to work hard," she replied, but somehow she sensed this "ideal" job might turn out to be more than she bargained for.

The food arrived and they ate in silence. She really was quite hungry now that she had had time to get over the disconcerting events of the day and evening.

When they had finished, and the elegant automobile was gliding along again, she started to direct him to her house, but he said that he knew where she lived and she settled back once more to enjoy a last few minutes of the night sky through the moon roof.

When they pulled into the narrow driveway behind the rather shabby Chevy that her family owned, she reached for the door handle. Then she paused and turned, "You said you wanted me to start tomorrow?"

"Yes, that's right. If you could come at, say eleven, you could get your belongings installed in your room and be ready to start at noon. Or, if you have no transportation, I could arrange to pick you up."

"I'm sure my mother can bring me. She seldom works on Saturday. If you'll give me directions to your house, please."

He furnished his address and she said, "I'll see you at eleven, then." She quickly got out of the car, walking toward the steps in the beam of the headlights.

Suddenly a lurching figure emerged from the kitchen door and a loud, slurring voice cut through the peace of the sleeping neighborhood. "That you, Molly?"

"Yes, Dad, I'm just getting home from work." Molly hurried forward, intending to get him into the house quickly before he said any more. But her hopes were dashed as he yelled, "Who's that in the car? Who the hell do you know that has a car like that?"

Please go, please go, she thought as she started up the steps.

But the car remained stubbornly in place, its piercing lights making sure its occupant missed nothing of the scene they illuminated.

"It's my boss, Dad, bringing me home from work. That's all."

"What kind of work, Molly? This late and a car like that – what kind of work, Molly?"

"Please, Dad, let's go inside and talk about it," she pleaded, but her words fell on deaf ears.

"Ain't just walking in here, you little –" and the words he used to finish the sentence brought flames to her face. She started up the steps, but he lurched forward and with outstretched arms gave her a push that caught her off balance. She grabbed the wobbly railing in an attempt to catch herself before she hit the pavement. It gave way, as it had been threatening to do for months, and she could feel herself falling. Before the hard ground could meet her plummeting body, a pair of strong arms caught her and brought her back onto her feet.

Before she knew what was happening, she had been deposited back in the car from the driver's side door and was shoved unceremoniously across the seat so that he could get in. Without a wasted movement, the car was reversed into the road and they were speeding down the street, which now had several lights glowing through the formerly dark windows. She could still hear her father hollering blessedly unintelligible words after them. Why, tonight of all nights, was he home before midnight?

She didn't say anything. What could she say that would dismiss that ugly scene from his mind, or hers? She just buried her face in her hands and let the tears of exhaustion, frustration and humiliation flow. She didn't see the grim determination on the face of the man beside her, or how his hands gripped the wheels so hard that the knuckles were white. She didn't see or feel anything but an overwhelming sense of despair, and the gamut of emotions she had experienced this long day seemed to drain from her body with her tears, leaving her numb and uncaring.

He didn't speak until, with a final shuddering sob, she fell back against the seat. Then his voice was almost gentle as he glanced at her ravished face. "Forget it, Molly. It won't happen again. We'll just move the schedule ahead a few hours. You can move into your new quarters tonight."

She nodded. She no longer really cared. It seemed she had lost complete control of her life and her destiny and it seemed a relief to have someone take charge and do her thinking for her. So she just sat quietly and let the man and the machine take her to whatever fate awaited.

She didn't pay any attention to where they were going, but knew they were ascending a rather steep and winding road. They slowed down and she noted that they were following a circular drive, going toward a white house which caught and reflected the approaching headlights. They continued past the columned front and drew up before one of the doors of the attached garage. Seemingly by magic, the door of the garage silently rose and they rolled into its dark interior. Almost immediately it filled with light and she blinked at its brightness after the pleasant darkness that had shielded her from the observant eyes beside her.

"Welcome home, Molly Stark," he said in a rather bemused voice.

"I apologize for tonight. I wish you hadn't seen my father like that."

His eyes fairly bored through her. "Are you saying that he's not always that, shall we say, unreasonable?"

"It's only when he's had too much to drink." She somehow felt a need to defend the father she sometimes resented so much, from this implacable man. "It's not always been like this, just since he lost his job."

"Did his drinking contribute to his losing it?"

"No, the drinking came afterward. It's been two years now and I think he's just discouraged."

"No matter what the circumstances, I see no excuse to physically assault and verbally abuse you. Now, let's go inside and get you settled for the night."

As Molly got out of the car, she noticed that the roomy garage contained another car as well as a garden tractor. They climbed a couple of steps to an enclosed breezeway and she waited while he unlocked the door at its far end. This led into a large modern kitchen decorated in white and royal blue with gleaming stainless steel appliances. One end was a work area and the other served as an informal dining space with white, wrought iron, glass topped table and blue cushioned wrought iron chairs sitting in front of a picture window which was framed in a profusion of climbing plants rather than curtains. Before she had time to absorb the lovely efficiency of this room, he was steering her on into the front hall. A curving staircase rose from its black and white marble floor and disappeared into the darkness above. The proceeded to the back of the hall, beneath the stairs where he opened a paneled door and flipping on the light switch, revealed a rather small, but charming bedsitting room.

The carpet was mauve and soft underfoot. The bed was made up like a couch with several plump mauve printed cushions and the French doors, that also served as the window to the room, had matching print drapes. A white wall unit provided desk, dressing table and storage space and white louvered doors obviously concealed a closet. He gestured toward another door on the far wall. "That's your bathroom."

"It's a lovely room," she said appreciatively.

"It's smallish, but adequate, I trust. It's been used on occasion as a guest room, so you should find the bathroom stocked with essentials for tonight. I'm afraid I can't provide any clothing at the moment, but I'm sure you can cope for what's left of tonight." He pointed toward the bedside table and she noticed for the first time, the white and brass, French style telephone. "Perhaps you can call your mother in the morning and have her deliver some things?"

"Yes, thank you. I'd like to relieve her worry tonight, but I'd better not call in case she has got my father quieted down. I wouldn't want to wake him." His words were spoken dryly. "I should think not. The address here is 101 Vista Heights, in case you'd forgotten in all the turmoil you've experienced tonight. Good night, Miss Stark. I'm sure a rest will make everything seem a bit brighter."

When he had closed the door and his firm step on the marble hall floor could no longer be heard, Molly opened the door that he had indicated was the bathroom, and noted with pleasure the small blue fixture cubicle with glass doored shower against mauve walls. The fluffy blue and mauve towels begged to have their softness enjoyed and she quickly stripped off her sticky, wilted uniform and jumped under the needles of hot water that spurted from the shower head at her command. The soap was fragrant and produced a think, velvety lather and she felt almost cleansed of her troubles as she stepped from the shower and wrapped the warm cloud of towel around her. She dried herself, and then wrapping a dry towel around her slender body, sarong style, turned out the lights and fell, exhausted, onto the welcoming bed.

HOUSEKEEPER DESIRED

She just noticed the waning orange moon looking in the French door as she closed her eyes and was lost in the world of healing oblivion.

2 CHAPTER TWO

Something touched her shoulder lightly. She shrugged it off, unready to return to the waking world. She felt the touch again and, annoyed, reached to brush it away. This time she was brought to full consciousness by the warm, firm hand that caught hers and squeezed it.

"Molly, wake up now." The voice was not loud, but very determined.

Resignedly, she forced open her heavy lids, then quickly closed them again at the invasion of the bright sunlight that was streaming into the room. The voice became quite firm. "Molly, you must wake up. Your mother's here."

"Mother?" She sat up abruptly, her towel sarong loosening dangerously. For a minute she stared at the tall, blond man standing over the bed. In the light of day, she noticed how the sun had streaked his hair with gold and how tan his skin was against the pale yellow shirt. His rather thin-lipped mouth was straight and looked capable of expressing any displeasure he might feel in a manner that would leave his victim in no doubt of his feelings.

"You must wake up. Come on before your mother suspects that what your father said last night might have some validity."

Molly flushed and was suddenly acutely aware of the maleness of the man she had thought of in completely sexless terms the day before. She clutched at the towel, and holding it tight across her thrusting breasts with one hand, sought to pull it over her long thighs with the other.

"What time is it?" she stammered.

"Almost ten."

"Oh, my, I am sorry! This is awful! I was supposed to start working today."

"It's all right. You really needed the rest and originally you were starting at noon, so you're far from late. When you hadn't stirred by nine, I called you mother and asked her to bring you a few things. I explained a little about last night, but I guess she overheard most of it anyway. I took the liberty of finding your phone number on the identification in your purse, since the number is not in the book. I hope you don't mind."

"No, it's quite all right. Thank you for going to the trouble, Mr. --, I still don't know your name!"

He walked casually to the door. I'll send your mother in."

He turned and faced her as he was about to open the door, "and the name is Stark, Molly, John Charles Stark. Considering the coincidence of our names being the same, I think you should call me J.C." He left her sitting there with her mouth slightly opened.

She hurried into the bathroom. When she emerged a few minutes later, her mother was waiting nervously in the center of the room, clutching a shabby suitcase in her hand.

"Hi, Mom. Thanks for bringing me my clothes. She dropped a light kiss on her mother's furrowed brow and gently disengaged her fingers from the handle of the luggage.

"Molly, I'm not sure I understand all of this, but I know you must have been terribly upset by your father last night."

Molly looked at her mother, standing there so bewilderedly in her rather tacky, polyester pants and top. Her brown hair had once been the same color as Molly's, but now was lusterless with touches of gray at the temples. She was only forty-two but the last two years had aged her a decade. Molly set the suitcase down and led her gently to the slipper chair by the French door.

"Sit down, Mom, and relax and I'll try to explain everything." Mrs. Stark sank wearily onto the chair, and it dawned on Molly that she had undoubtedly had much less rest last night than she, herself, had had. At least Molly had been whisked away from all the mess and had been deposited in a comfortable, luxurious room, while Mrs. Stark had had to suffer the abuse of the very drunk husband and live with the knowledge that the neighbors and her other children had been spared none of it. She was the one that had to face all of them in the light of day, and even though it wasn't her fault, she was the type that would apologize for her husband's behavior to all them, and would make the inevitable excuses for him.

"I found out about this job yesterday, quite by accident. Mr. Stark called to inquire about your availability and I knew you wouldn't be able to leave home. It pays more than my other two jobs together, and seemed ideal. You'll have one less mouth to feed at home and I can give you just as much money, maybe more. Mr. Stark really wanted someone older, more mature, but he's giving me a chance to prove myself and I really think I can handle the job."

Mrs. Stark nodded. "I know all about that Molly. He came to the house yesterday after he talked with you. He wanted to know all about you and he stayed for quite some time. Your father wasn't home, thank goodness. He was very nice and seems like a decent man. But are you sure that you can do all that is required in a house this size and with entertaining and all?"

"I've got to try, Mom, and you now that I'm used to long hours and seven days a week. At least here I'll have one whole and two half days off."

"I know how hard you've worked, Molly, and I'm sorry it's had to be that way. I know many daughters wouldn't be willing to waste their youth doing what you've done. But your father will find a job or get called back soon. I know he will. And then you can go back to school and we'll be a happy, normal family again."

"Sure, Mom." Molly replied, but she thought about how many times in the past two years she had heard those very words. She guessed if her mother gave up that hope, then there wouldn't be much left for her.

Her mother got to her feet. "I must get back before your father wakes up. We'll miss you a lot, Molly."

"I'll come home on days off and I'm sure there will be lots of odd hours when I can drop in for a while. Any time you need me, there's the phone."

"It just won't be the same," she said wistfully and with a half-hearted smile she left.

Molly placed the suitcase on the bed and pulled out undies, a pair of blue cotton slacks and a matching knit shirt. She dressed quickly and ran a comb through her hair. A dash of lipstick added a bit of color to her rather pale face. She grimaced as she looked at herself in the mirror. Maybe she would have a little time to get out in the sun with this job, and she thought about the color of Mr. Stark's skin compared to hers. Then she stood up straight, held her chin up proudly and went out to face the world, which this morning consisted of this gorgeous house and J.C. Stark, who she suddenly realized was pretty gorgeous himself.

The marble floor of the hall gleamed in the sunlight streaming in through the fan-shaped window over the big white front door and she noted with delight the paintings of the same covered bridge done in each of the four seasons of the year that were the only adornment on the stark white walls. The frames were gilt and black and quite ornate. An oval, marble-topped table at the foot of the stairs was the only piece of furniture and on it was a French styled phone in gleaming brass.

The kitchen was even more wonderful than she remembered from her brief glimpse the night before. It was large, light and airy and she noticed that the royal blue and white color scheme was accented with lemon yellow. An identical window to the one by the table was over the sink and counter. It, too, was framed in plants rather than curtains. She had never seen a prettier, more perfect kitchen, not even in a magazine.

So busy was she, takin in all the details of her new surroundings, that she did not notice her new boss until he spoke.

"You approve of my home, I trust."

Molly turned guiltily from her close examination of the room. "What I've seen so far is exquisite, Mr. Star- J.C. I didn't see much last night, I'm afraid. I really do love this kitchen, and the hall is just lovely and my room, too."

"We'll take a tour presently, but why don't you sit down now and drink this coffee I've poured before it gets cold and then, have some breakfast. You must be hungry after your meager diet of yesterday."

J.C. had addressed her from his seat at the table. A large blue mug of coffee was in front of him and one of the same proportions in lemon yellow was sitting opposite him, steam rising from its contents. She slipped into the chair across from him and took a tentative sip.

"You make good coffee," she announced.

"A man alone has to be self-sufficient. I don't expect to have to make my own from now on, except on your day off. Besides," and he grinned wickedly, "one can hardly miss with the automatic machine."

"I'm eager to try out all the marvelous appliances. I'm used to doing things with a lot less equipment than I see here. I hope I can run them all properly."

"I'm sure that you can. Modern ladies seem to have a way with machines."

They finished their coffee and he insisted that she at least have an English muffin or some toast. She decided on the former and popped two into the broiler oven on the counter. While they were browning, she refilled the coffee cups and got out butter and some raspberry jam that was in the refrigerator. She spread the hot muffins lavishly with the butter and jam, put them on small plates and placed one before him as well as at her own place.

"That looks like the kind of sandwich I used to make when I was a kid," he observed. "All butter and jam with a little bread."

"Did I overdo it?" she asked anxiously. "I like them that way myself and I never thought to ask if you did, too."

"Yes, I suppose you could say it's overdone, Molly, but that's the way I like them too."

She gave a little sigh of relief.

"Now let's go over some of the details of the job while we enjoy this wickedly rich snack." He savored a bite of the buttery, sweet muffin and the continued. "What I need is a woman to oversee the care of my home, do the cooking and attend to little details, like shopping, running to the cleaners and the like. I entertain or have house guests from time to time and I need a person capable of planning and providing meals and, in general, to see to their comfort. I do not expect that everything can be done single-handed, but I do expect that much of it will be, and what can't be, will be seen to by additional help which you will seek and hire. That would include caterers or kitchen help when there is a large party, carpet shampooers, window washers and the like. There is already a cleaning lady who comes every Friday and will do the heavier cleaning. I also have a man who does the lawns and gardens and comes one or more days a week depending on the weather and the time of year. I am away frequently as my business is headquartered in Boston and involves several other locations in Massachusetts and southern New Hampshire. I prefer to have the house occupied while I'm away. There are phone calls to handle and messages to record and the occasional letter to be typed, though I have most of that sort of thing done at the office."

He paused and looked at Molly, who was thinking that what he had given as a job description, sounded might like the duties of a wife, but who said, "It sounds quite challenging, J.C., but I think, given a chance to become familiar with the house and your preferences, I can handle it. I am looking forward to trying."

"Another thing, Molly. Since you are undertaking a job most usually entrusted to a much more mature person, in years anyway, I think it would be best for your image and mine if you would wear skirts or dresses, while on duty, so to speak."

Molly reddened as she looked down ruefully at the casual sporty slacks and shirt she was wearing. She hadn't given clothing a thought and she realized that her wardrobe consisted of very little except slacks, jeans and the numerous leotards required for her salon job. She did have two waitress uniforms, but they were cheap, ugly and well worn. She just couldn't were them in this elegant house. The denim skirt might do for mornings and working about the house. What would she do about entertaining?

As if he could read her thoughts, J.C. added, "Since I am requiring a certain dress code, I expect to provide some of the clothing. This afternoon would be as good a time as any to take care of that detail." He consulted his watch, which was thin and gold and matched the sun-bleached hair on his muscular arm. J.C. Stark might be a business man, but he was in superb physical condition, observed Molly, who was very conscious of posture and muscle tone due to her job at the salon. "now if you've finished eating, we'll tour the house and then you can clean up the kitchen, your room and mine and we'll head for the shops at, say, noon."

"Won't you require some lunch?"

"Since we are getting a rather late start today and since there are so many things for you to become familiar with, I think that we would be advised to have something in town when we finish the shopping. Now, you've seen the kitchen, so let's go through the rest of the house." He stood up, his height surprising her each time she found herself sitting while he stood. His long legs were clad in light beige, casual slacks that fit him to perfection, accenting the muscular but trim thighs without appearing too tight. He didn't miss her assessment, but rather added his own of her tall graceful form as she stood to follow him.

White louvered doors in the north wall of the kitchen were folded open to reveal a small laundry room with washer, dryer, cupboards and counter and a fold-away ironing board. It was done in the same color scheme as the kitchen and the one high window was also framed by climbing plants. Molly noted that she would have to get some expert advise on watering and caring for them. A door at the right of the laundry room revealed another small room which contained an upright freezer and several cupboards and closets for storing food and extra supplies for cleaning and the general upkeep of a house this size. She noted with satisfaction that the shelves were quite well stocked.

Across the hall from the kitchen was the L shaped living room. The narrower part of the L was as you entered, leaving room for a dining room of perfect proportions for seating eight or ten people. The stepped into the dining room. The carpet was blue oriental with lots of soft beige and the pecan dining room table was flanked by four matching chairs on either side and one at each end. The blue and beige tapestry seats of the chairs caught and held the same hues as the carpet. The small crystal chandelier that was suspended over the dining room table was elegant without being overly ornate. A sideboard on one side of the room displayed assorted pieces of silver that reflected the rest of the room as a series of mirrors would and a curved front, glass doored china cabinet on the other side held breathtakingly beautiful pieces of china and blue glassware. The French doors at the end of the room also served as the windows and were flanked on either side by blue velvet draperies which could be drawn across them at night or to keep out the sun on a hot day.

"It's very lovely," Molly breathed.

"I'm glad you like it," he replied. "Now let's go into the living room. You an explore the sideboard for table linens and such when we have more time."

Back in the living room, Molly drank in the quiet beauty of the huge room. From the deep red carpet that cushioned her feet to the off white walls and black marble fireplace, the room was a symphony of elegance and comfort. The sofas that faced each other in front of the fireplace were off white velvet with plump read and pearl gray velvet pillows arranged invitingly. A low ebony table with an ivory inlaid top sat between the two sofas. Queen

Anne styled chairs, upholstered in deep red and off white velvet, were placed strategically around the room, some flanked by tables and others by tall oriental vases. Two sets of French doors formed one end of the room, with a large multi-paned window facing the front lawn at the other end. The slubbed silk draperies on both were the same shade of white as the walls. Above the marble mantle hung a seascape at sunset, and the art objects on the mantle were ginger jars and pieces of ivory and jade that had been carefully chosen to enhance the piece of art that hung above them.

Molly felt almost overwhelmed by the rich surroundings in which she found herself. She had assumed that her employer was quite well to do, as the ordinary person just didn't hire full time household help, but the obvious luxury displayed here, was even more than she had anticipated. When he spoke, it brought her out of her reverie with a start.

"You approve?" His voice was almost cynical. She know that he had visited her own modest, no, shabby, home and flushed slightly.

"It's so very nice." Then she thought how stupid that remark must sound coming from a poor girl like herself. "What I mean is," she stammered, "it's quite overwhelming to me actually. As you know, I am not used to such elegant surroundings."

"I am sure you can adapt quite nicely. Now we'll just step through this door into my den." He opened a paneled door in the far wall and they entered a room that was more of an office than anything else. Walnut wainscoting reached half way up the walls and was topped by beige burlap. The two windows were multi-paned and the drapes were soft coral in a rough textured fabric. The room was dominated by a large curved front walnut desk, behind which was a rich brown upholstered swivel chair. A smaller desk with typewriter sat under the window and several wooden file cabinets stood against another wall. The carpet was short shag in a tweed of beige, dark brown and coral.

J.C. pointed to a door to the left and behind the desk. "That leads to my inner sanctum. You can check it out some other time. Now let's go upstairs and look at the bedrooms"

Mutely, Molly followed the long stride in the beige slacks back across the living room and up the curving stairs, which were carpeted in red oriental and mad no sound under their feet as they climbed the graceful flight to the second story of the house. The white walls were graced here and there with watercolors framed in the same black and gold as the paintings in the downstairs hall and the long hall at the top of the staircase was carpeted with the same oriental print. There were four paneled doors, one at each end and two in the middle of the hallway. She followed him to the far left and he announced, as he threw open the door, "This is my room and the only one that will have to be done every day, when I'm home, that is."

She stepped past him, feeling almost like she was invading a very private part of his life, and took in the obviously masculine room. The light beige carpet and velvet drapes were the same color as the walls and the king size brass bed which was unmade, had beige sheets and a chocolate brown spread. Brass and glass end tables repeated the glow of the headboard and held tall slender brass lamps with very modern domed white glass shades, a gold and brown leaf print along the edges, softening their severity. A velvet chair and ottoman in bronze, and a chest and armoire in some dark wood with brass handles completed the furnishings. The louvered doors on the right wall obviously concealed the closet and he opened another paneled door to reveal generous sized bathroom with dark brown fixtures and beige tiled floor and walls. The towels were the same thick, thirsty kind that she had found in her own bath, but in beige and chocolate.

They proceeded to the next room down the hall, where a bedroom as feminine as his was masculine, was revealed for her observation. The white and gold French provincial furniture was set off by pale blue carpeting, walls, drapes and spread. An adjoining bathroom was decorated in gold and yellow and also connected to the third bedroom which was quite masculine with its sleigh bed, lack of frills and moss green color scheme. The fourth room was as large as J.C.'s and done in palest silver gray with a dusty rose velvet spread. Indeed, the room was almost a duplicate of his, except for the color scheme and the fact that the headboard and end tables were chrome and glass rather than brass, and that the choice of rose made it an infinitely more feminine room than his. The bath with this room was by far the most elegant that she had seen, with pink fixtures set in a background of black marble and the tube was a sunken one. The towels were rose and pale gray. One whole wall was mirrored and she could almost see herself luxuriating in the enormous tub and the stepping out to wrap her body in a huge towel as she pirouetted before the mirrored wall. She felt the color rise to her face as J.C. watched her with a bemused expression on his face, rather like he could read her thoughts as clearly as if they were printed across her smooth brow.

"This is the loveliest house I have ever seen," she said "Taking care of it should be a pleasure."

"I find it suits my needs when I am here very well and since I purchased it, about a year ago, I have found myself spending more and more time here, particularly in the summer and fall. A friend helped me with the decorating and her tastes and mine seemed to coincide or at least blend quite well."

So there was a lady in his life, one close enough to entrust with decorating his home. She should have known that. There could be no way that a handsome, successful man like he was, would be alone in the world. She wondered what she looked like.. Surely she would be as beautiful and elegant as the surroundings she had helped to create. Molly found herself feeling a little envious of this mystery "friend".

"Come, let's you and I get to work and then we'll go shopping. You can do what needs to be done in the kitchen, make my bed and do your own unpacking while I go to my den to take care of some phone calls and such."

"Since we're up here, I'll start with the bedroom I think."

"Fine. We'll meet in the hall in one hour then." He left the room with his purposeful stride and Molly went back down the hall to his room. She quickly made the bed and picked up the pieces of clothing from the chair, hanging some in the spacious closet and depositing the socks, shirt and underwear in a little pile by the door to take downstairs and wash. She lingered for a moment by the French doors which opened onto a little balcony overlooking the pool and patio in the back yard. Then she proceeded to put away the toilet articles on the sink and counter in the bathroom and gather up the used towels.

She took the bundle of soiled clothing and towels dow to the laundry room and started the washer. It didn't take long to clean up the remains of their scanty breakfast and then she headed back to her own room.

The enormous closet looked almost as empty with her few belongings in it as it had before she unpacked. And the well worn articles of clothing looked rather like rummage sale rejects hanging in the lovely surroundings. She sighed and closed the closet door. The little clock on the bedside table indicated that she had a few minutes before their appointed time to meet, so she changed the offensive slacks for a denim wrap skirt and checked blouse. She loosened her hair from the black ribbon which constrained it and brushed it until it flipped up on the ends that just fell short of her shoulders. She repaired her lipstick and added a touch of mascara to the long lashes. I do look like a country cousin, she thought, but it's the best I can do with fifteen minutes and what I have to work with. Why she cared so much about her looks, she didn't know, except that she was going to be seen with this tall, handsome man who was so obviously used to only the best. I don't want to be an embarrassment, she told herself. As she stepped out into the front hall one minute before the hour, she found him already standing there, glancing at his watch with seeming impatience. Evidently promptness was on of his virtues and she surmised that he would accept no less from his employees, unless the circumstances were extremely extenuating.

"I'm ready," she announced and he gave her a brief, surface smile as his eyes did a quick assessment from top to bottom.

"Yes, and on time, too. Let's go then."

Molly preceded him through the kitchen and breezeway to the garage. When she stopped by the vehicle they had used the previous night, he kept on going and threw back over his shoulder, "We'll take the Saab today and since you will be using this car to do the shopping and such, you will drive."

So he wanted to see how well she could drive. That was one test she knew she could pass. Molly liked driving, though she rarely had the family car to use, and the thought of driving this sleek little blue car delighted her. The bucket seats were the same shade of blue as the exterior of the car and she felt quite comfortable after she had adjusted the seat forward a little. Here legs were long and she drove in a position back from the wheel, but his were much longer and he had obviously been the last one to drive it.

When he was seated, J.C. handed her the keys and pushed the automatic garage door opener. The engine purred to life beneath her hands and she backed smoothly out onto the wide driveway. She would have liked to have taken in the view of the house and its landscaping in the light of day, but sensed his impatience to be off and recognized the need to concentrate on what she was doing in a strange car and under such careful observation.

They rolled down the drive and, after stopping, onto the winding, downhill road that led to the main highway. They passed four houses on the way down, all widely spaced with lovely lawns and gardens. The main road was the one leading into the center of the town and she recognized where she was from the shopping center that was almost directly across the road from them. She made a right turn and headed for the main street.

"Where are we going?" she asked.

"I made some inquiries this morning and it seems that there is a shop called Ms. That should suit us for finding what we need." Then as an afterthought, "Of course, if you know of a better place, we could go there instead."

"No, I don't know of a better ladies' store. I rarely go there because it is very expensive, but if you think…"

"Then Ms. it is. I shall decide on what's too expensive and what isn't, seeing as I am paying the bill."

"Of course," she said in a low tight-lipped voice. Again she could feel her face redden and whished that there were a way to control the involuntary color that always flushed her face when she became embarrassed, angry or confused.

As always on a Saturday, the streets were swarming with cars and pedestrians and one had to concentrate on what one was doing, so neither of them spoke until she found a parking place quite close to the store he had mentioned and pulled into it. She took the keys from the ignition and held them out to him.

"Keep that set, Molly. You are a very competent driver and I'm quite satisfied that you can handle this car very nicely. Consider this your car to drive for any errands and you may use it for your days off, as well, unless I have a need for it."

"Thank you. That is very generous of you."

"I am sure it is to my advantage not to have to be concerned with picking up groceries, cleaning and the like and not to have to give you rides here and there."

Damn! Here came that hot, red flush to her face again.

The interior of the store was cool and seemed almost dark after the brightness of the July sun outside. There were a few customers surveying the racks of clothes against the walls and three chicly dressed and coiffured salesgirls were hovering at a discreet distance, ready to be of service, should any of them need help. J.C. loomed tall and overwhelmingly male in the very female atmosphere and Molly noticed that all three store employees noticed their entrance. The most mature looking of the three, and probably the one in charge, immediately turned her attention from the other customers and sailed across the thick blue carpet toward them. Her black sundress fit to perfection and the crisp white jacket and fashionable hairdo made her look cool and unflappable. Molly felt quite rumpled and dowdy in comparison.

Her smile was charmingly professional as she directed her remark to Molly, but made it quite obvious that her mind was on the tall, handsome man beside her. "May I help you?"

Before Molly could think of what to say, she was rescued by his response. "The lady will require two or three skirts and blouses and a couple of dresses. Would you be kind enough to show her what you have in her size?"

Slowly the clerk withdrew her eyes from the contact of those of the rare male customer and quickly scanned the tall, slender form of the girl beside him.

"We have several choices that should fit madam... Follow me please." She led them to a rack of skirts and pointed out the section in Molly's size. There were several and Molly would have liked to have spent a long time looking and choosing, but she felt that she must not hold J.C. up for long. Instinct told her this was not something he was in the habit of doing and was undoubtedly not where he would prefer being right now. Her practical side took over and she quickly disregarded the gay, voguish, prints and settled on a navy wrap skirt that reversed to a small scale print in blue white and red, a white pleated one and a softly gathered one in beige with black and white stripes in irregular widths and sporting large patch pockets. She already had a suitable white top, so she chose red, black and turquoise blouses. She followed the clerk to the dressing room and with as much speed as possible, tried on the clothing she had selected. She was quite pleased with her choices and all fit her well. She was about to don her old clothes again, when there was a knock on the door.

"Yes?" she said.

The voice of the saleslady replied, "Here are some dresses that your husband thought you might like. Would you try them on please?"

Molly started to say that he was not her husband and then thought better of it. What could she say he was that would not meet with a knowing look? So she opened the door and bit and reached out for the dresses. One was a plain light blue knit with a t-shirt style top and a self belt. The other was a print in pink and white silk that felt weightless on her body. The fit to perfection, even the length. Molly surveyed herself admiringly in the full length mirror in the silk. The she looked at the tag and gasped when she saw the price. She quickly took it off and put on the denim skirt and shirt, gathered up the clothing she had tried on and went out to join J.C. and the saleslady.

He looked at her with her arms laden with garments and hangers, then quickly stepped forward to relieve her of her burden.

"I had hoped you'd model the dresses for me. Didn't they fit?"

"Oh, yes, they fit beautifully."

"Good, then we shall have these as well as the other things."

The clerk beamed as she started takin the garments to the counter to ring up the sale and wrap them.

"J.C. I really don't feel you should buy me the dresses. They are very costly and I'm sure that I won't need..."

"Let me be the judge of that please, Molly. There will be occasions in the evening when I am entertaining that will require that sort of thing. I am sure you would want to wear the appropriate thing."

"Yes, of course."

When the new garments were boxed and bagged, they stored them in the trunk of the car and J.C. suggested that they have lunch in a nearby restaurant.

He took the opportunity to elaborate on the duties that he expected her to undertake and she wished she had something to make notes on as his list of instructions grew. She took careful notice of his choices from the luncheon menu so that she would have some idea of his likes when it came to preparing food, but as much as she tried to learn about him, she had the feeling that he was finding out more about her in the same length of time and with very little questioning.

The food was delicious and if she could have felt more relaxed, she would have enjoyed it tremendously, but this man across from her was a very disturbing individual. She felt that if she let her guard down for a minute she would do or say something that would cause that betraying flush to suffuse her face. So she ate slowly and carefully and made as few comments as possible, and let him do most of the talking.

3 CHAPTER THREE

J.C. did the driving on the return trip and Molly had an opportunity to take in the exterior of the house more fully. The paved drive cut a dark circle in the lush green expanse of lawn. The circle that it enveloped was studded with bright flower beds like pieces of cloisonné on black cord. The perfect symmetry of blue spruce trees graced the entrance to the drive. The house was long and white with narrow square pillars supporting the roof of a portico above the flagstone front terrace. Since it was at the very top of the hill, it commanded a view in every direction of mountains and valleys and the many tones and shades of green that make up the hills of western New Hampshire. She thought about how breathtaking it must be in the autumn when the leaves blazed with color.

J.C. parked the car by the front door this time and they carried the purchases they had made into Molly's room. After depositing the boxes and bags on her bed, he suggested that after she had put her clothes away she might like to make a trip home to get more of her belongings.

"I think I could use some more things, especially shoes which Mother didn't think to bring," she said. "But I must dry the clothes I left washing and start dinner soon. I don't have to do it right now."

J.C. frowned. "Is it your habit to argue over every suggestion that is made to you?"

If her face was as red as the heat that swept over her face this time, then she must be almost purple. "No, I don't intend to argue. I didn't think of it that way. I just don't want to take advantage and I'm thinking of my job first. That's all. I'm sorry if I seem to be balky or ungrateful."

His voice softened as he said, "Don't worry, Molly. You are prone to fretting, I'm afraid, and I can see why. But I'll let you know if you are not doing a satisfactory job. I told you that I would give you a fair trial and in two weeks we should both know if it's going to work out or not."

"That seems very fair."

"Very well, carry on then. When you get back you can make a light meal for us. 6:30 would be a good time for me as I have an engagement this evening. Since there are no guests, I'd as soon eat with you in the kitchen. We'll use the dining room any time there's company."

Molly stood for a minute looking at the door through which he had just departed. He had been almost angry with her and she sensed that should that anger become unleashed, it could be quite devastating to the person on whose head it might fall.

She carefully hung the new clothes in the closet and finding her keys in her purse headed out to the car. She was just about to get in when she remembered the wash. Running back to the laundry, she quickly transferred the wet clothes to the dryer and then was on her way again.

Her pleasure at driving the car was marred by the thought of what she would have to face when she got home. She hoped that her father wouldn't be there, but knew that she'd have to face him sooner or later. If he were sober, there would be no problem, but that wasn't too likely. It was only a matter of ten minutes drive to go from the luxury of the hill top paradise of J. C. Stark to the modest neighborhood and unpretentious house that Molly called home. She noticed how badly the one and a half story frame needed paint and why hadn't Mike done something about the over long, weed ridden lawn when he took care of other lawns?

The car was not in the yard, which meant that either her father or mother or both were away. Se rather hoped that it was the former. She climbed the porch steps slowly and opening the screen door said tentatively, "Anybody home?"

She could hear the television set going and went through the empty kitchen into the front hallway. She peered into the living room. Mike was slumped in the recliner watching a baseball game.

"How come you're not mowing the lawn? It sure needs it." she announced.

Mike sat up with a start. "Sis, where did you come from ? Mom said you weren't going to live with us anymore."

"Well, I am going to be living where I'm working, but I do plan to come home now and then. It's only right here in town you know."

He grinned. "I'm glad of that. It seemed awful lonesome without you here this morning and after last night. Boy, was Dad on a tear. I wish I could move out, too, sometimes."

Molly walked into the room and put her arm around Mike's shoulder. "Mike, I know it isn't easy, but you're just a kid yet and Mom and Maria need you. Please don't think about doing anything rash. It'll get better, you'll see."

Mike's candid brown eyes met hers, "That's what I've been hearing forever around here. When I'm sixteen I'm going to get a job and get out of here."

"That's four years yet, Mike. And you mustn't thin about not finishing school. Promise me that you won't do anything rash without talking to me about it first."

Mike's face showed his doubt about her words, but he mumbled begrudgingly, "Okay, Sis. I promise."

She hugged him and said, "I know you won't let me down. Where's Mom?"

"She said she had to get some groceries. Maybe she's looking for Dad, too. He woke up this morning in a real bad mood and Mom wasn't here and he took off. She was really upset when she got back and he wasn't here."

"Oh, darn. That's my fault. She brought me some clothes this morning and she seemed afraid that the might wake up before she got back."

"Maria had already gone to work so I was the only one here. He started saying some awful things about you, so I just left."

"He was so drunk last night. I thought he'd have forgotten what he did and said last night."

"Well, he didn't and I couldn't listen to him any more."

"I'm sorry, Mike. This new job seemed like such a good deal for me and for the family as I'll make more money. But maybe I made a mistake. Mom is down and Dad is causing you all more grief that before. Maybe I should work out a notice."

Mike sighed. "Don't do it, Sis. We sure would like to have you back here, but with the way Dad is acting, you'd be miserable. Maybe I'm just a kid, but I know what you've already given up to help out and I wouldn't do it if I had the chance to get out."

"You might be just a kid, Mike, but you're a good one and you've had to grow up a lot faster than most. Now I'm going up to get a few things and then I have to get back to start dinner."

Molly hurried up the stairs to her room and quickly selected the clothing, shoes and cosmetic items she would need. She put the shoes in her old gym bag and went to the kitchen for some paper bags for the remaining things. Her mother drove in just as she was about to return to her room. Molly went to the door and held it open for the parcel laden, dragging woman.

"Molly, what are you doing here? I couldn't imagine whose car was in the yard."

"It's my boss's car. I came home to get a few more things I need."

Mrs. Stark put the packages on the table and sat down in one of the chrome chairs. Molly had seen her mother look distraught before, but today was worse than ever. She went to the stove and put the tea kettle on.

"Mike says Dad was still upset with me this morning."

"I haven't seen him, Molly. I'm worried. I checked all his old haunts and no one has seen him today."

"He'll come back, Mom. He always does."

Mrs. Stark let out a shuddering sigh and Molly knew that she was battling tears. "I hope you're right, Molly. We've been married for twenty-two years and I really do love him. A lot of those years, in fact most of them, were very happy and loving ones. I know a lot of people think I should leave him and all but I just can't desert him now when he is not in control of himself. If he had a bad illness, I'd certainly not leave him and this is the same sort of thing really."

Molly laid her hand on her mother's bowed head. "I know how you feel, Mom. I only wish I could do more to help. It seems now that, without meaning to, I've worsened things."

"No, you haven't really, Molly. You're just the one that his is venting all his frustrations on right now. Do what you have to do and we'll hope for the best."

HOUSEKEEPER DESIRED

The kettle began to whistle and Molly made her mother a cup of tea. "I wish I could sit here and have one with you, Mom, but I have to finish packing up and get back so I can have dinner ready on time."

"I understand, Dear. Go right ahead. Do you need any help?"

"No, there isn't that much that I'm taking. It's all ready to go. I just came down to get some bags."

She quickly packed up her belongings, adding her jewelry box and bathing suit and hollered down the stairs for Mike to come up and help put it in the car. Back in the kitchen, she dropped a kiss on her mother's cheek and said that she knew her father would be home soon. Then she hurried out to the car, which Mike was checking out with love lights in his eyes.

"What a car, Sis! I'll bet you like driving this baby after our old clunker!"

"It's super to drive, Mike, but I'd settle for something a lot less wonderful if it were my own."

"Well, I'm going to have one of these someday, you wait and see."

"I hope you do, Mike. Now look after Mom, and do something about that lawn and if you need anything, call me."

"Sure, Sis. Will we be seeing you again soon?"

"My full day off is Wednesday. I'll stop by for a while then."

"Okay, Sis, and good luck."

Molly backed out into the street and waved as she drove off. She was not happy about leaving her mother in the state she was in, but she had to succeed in her new job and starting her first day with a late dinner was not the way to do it.

When Molly entered the house via the breezeway and kitchen. J.C. was not in evidence, so she made two quick trips from the car to her room with her belongings. She could put them away after dinner when J.C. said he'd be out. She whipped off the denim skirt and started to shed her blouse when she looked out the French door of her room and was more than a little chagrined to see J.C. just pulling himself out of the pool. Had he seen her? There was no way to tell. She darted quickly to the window and pulled the drapes across, leaving the room in the soft light that glowed through them. Then she hastily shed the rest of her garments and took a refreshing shower.

The new beige striped skirt and black top made her feel almost like a new person and she went to the kitchen to see what she could find that would be easy to fix and yet tasty and satisfying. She made a fresh fruit salad and thawed some frozen chicken breasts in the microwave, which she then proceeded to pound flat and brown before adding a wine sauce and popping into the oven. She steamed some asparagus that she found in the freezer and made a batch of biscuits from her mother's recipe which always turned out light as a feather. If he wanted dessert tonight, she thought, he'd have to settle for ice cream with crème de menth.

At six-thirty on the dot, J.C. came into the kitchen sniffing the air appreciatively. "If the food tastes as good as it smells, you're in good shape, Molly." He announced and then added with a little grin, "Well, let's say you're in fine shape anyway"

Could he be referring to the open drapes when she started disrobing, she wondered, or was it just a casual compliment? She busied herself with arranging the chicken and biscuits on serving plates so that she hoped he wouldn't notice her guilty look. He took his seat at the table and when she had finished putting all the food on, she sat across from him and they began eating.

After he had savored the first few bites, he asked casually, "How are things at home today?"

"Not very good. My father left while my mother was here and she can't find him."

"I'm not sure that she should try."

"She loves him very much and she is concerned about him. It's very hard to explain to someone that didn't know him before."

"You're right, of course. It's just that I realy can't abide the type of behavior he exhibited last night and had I not been there, you might have been badly hurt."

Molly thought to herself that if she hadn't met and gone home with him, then her father would not have been in such a fury or had the suspicions he was so loudly broadcasting, but she kept quiet and went on eating.

When they had finished the chicken and he had eaten several of the biscuits, she asked if he would care for dessert.

"No, I think the number of biscuits I ate should stick with me for some time. They were really excellent, Molly, and obviously made from scratch."

She flushed slightly at his praise and said, "It's a recipe my mother always uses and is quite quick and easy. The are good hot, and cold they make a marvelous shortcake."

"Do we have any left?"

"Oh, yes, I made a dozen and you haven't eaten nearly that many."

"Then please demonstrate their use in a shortcake for dinner tomorrow, which, by the way, I would like around one as I will need to head for Boston later in the afternoon." J.C. stood, patted his stomach which was flat as a pancake, smiled and said, "I don't know if I can afford to keep you or not, Molly Stark. If I continue to eat like this, I will soon look like your, Mr. Gresham I believe it was?"

Molly had to grin at the thought of the short, fat Gresham in comparison to this tall, trim man before here, and thought it would take a lot more than obesity for him to bear any resemblance to her former employer. "I'll try to keep the calories down a bit if you wish," she said. "Good food doesn't have to be that fattening and at the salon we were required to instruct in good nutrition while losing weight."

"I'll leave that up to you, but I do not wish to be put on a rabbit food diet just yet."

J.C. went upstairs to dress for his engagement and she wondered if it was with the mysterious Joan who had helped him decorate this house. While she cleared the table and stacked the dishwasher, she tried to picture what she would look like. Would he choose tall and graceful or petit? Blonde or dark, or maybe with hair the color of autumn leaves on a sugar maple? Would she be athletic, as he obviously was, or a hot house lily? She had good taste and an eye for color and design, as was evidenced in the house. Maybe she was a decorator?

When the kitchen looked as untouched as it had the first time she saw it, she went to her room to put away her possessions. The clothes she added to the closet made it about one third full with plenty of room between the garments so that they wouldn't crush. Her undies and other items took only two of the six generously sized drawers in the wall unit, but if she stayed on she would be adding her fall and winter things. When she had finished, she realized that the only item showing that was her personal belonging was the jewelry box on the dressing table. She decided that when she got her first pay check she would buy something of her own to add to the room like a small figurine that would be of her choosing but blend with the setting, or maybe a nice brass picture frame or tow to display some of her family's pictures in.

There was a light tap at her door and at her, "Come in," J.C. opened the door and entered. "I forgot to mention a couple of things, Molly. He slid open a panel of the wall unit to display a television set and small sterio unit. "You have these to help entertain you when you're not working and feel free to use the pool. You do swim?"

"Yes, I'm a good swimmer. I have my life saving certificate and worked as a guard at a public pool when I was in high school."

"I somehow thought you would be good at sports. It is possible that I will have some calls while I'm out. Most of them required you to just take a number or a message, but if Ben Adams should call, there is a number beside the hall phone where I can be reached. Please don't give it to anyone else."

"That seems easy enough."

"Oh, by the way. There are two phone lines to the house. Yours, the kitchen and guest rooms are on one line and the hall, my den and my bedroom are on another. If you are going to be in your room, you might leave the door open so you'll hear it ring in the hall. If you go swimming or outdoors, take the portable phone in my inner sanctum with you. It will reach to several hundred feet from the house."

"I will. Have a good time. What time shall I fix breakfast?"

"You are the practical one, aren't you? Shall we say nine? I may be quite late and I'm sure you won't be eager to get up too early on Sunday."

"That sounds fine," and her eyes followed his striking form in the superbly tailored light gray slacks and blue blazer as he disappeared through her doorway. She felt just a little lonesome and very envious of the lady that he would be taking to some nice place she felt sure.

She fiddled idly with the television set and found nothing to hold her interest, so she wandered out into the living room and did a more careful examination of its treasures. Then she remembered his so called inner sanctum and decided to explore it. She opened the door he had pointed out on the back wall of his den and stepped through into a room of about the same size but not at all businesslike in appearance. The walls, windows and carpets were the same, but the furniture consisted of a soft leather sofa and the biggest recliner she had ever seen. There was a large television set and a small bar, complete with sink and refrigerator. One cluster of photographs on the wall must be of family members and another were autographed and must be of sports and political figures. A glassed in bookcase on one wall held several trophies and a number of books, annuals, and what appeared to be scrap books and photo albums. This room also had a French door to the back patio and pool, but the drape was pulled across it like he didn't want any invasion into this private relaxing place. She spotted the portable phone on the table beside the recliner and took it with her as she suddenly felt like a swim.

Her turquoise bikini on, she slipped out the French door of her room and headed for the pool. Its interior was painted sky blue and the water looked cool and refreshing. Placing the phone on the glass topped table beneath the blue and yellow umbrella, she stepped out onto the board and dove cleanly into the water. It felt quite cool at first, then caressed her body like liquid satin as she swam several lengths, before turning over to float on her back. As she pulled herself out of the pool, the phone rang; not the piercing ring of the ordinary phone, but a half ring, half buzz. She picked it up, pushed the required button and said, "Hello."

The strident female voice that met her ear made her move the phone away from her a few inches. "Who is this?" it demanded, rather than asked.

"This is Molly Stark speaking."

"Who are you? Are you a relative of John's?"

Molly almost told the caller that she had a wrong number and then remembered that he was probably John to everyone else and that she was perhaps the only one who thought of him as J.C.

"No, I'm the housekeeper. Our last names are only a coincidence. Mr. Stark is away this evening. Can I take a message?"

"Damn, I wanted to talk to him. Where is he?"

"He didn't say where he was going," Molly said truthfully.

"Well, will he be back soon?"

"I think he expects to be out rather late, Mrs --," and Molly paused, hoping the person on the other end would fill in the blank.

"It's Miss Drew" and she accented the Miss, "Dina Drew and I'm sure that John would want me to have a number where he can be reached."

Molly hated to lie, but J.C. had been very definite in his instructions about the use of the number he had left.

"I'm sorry Miss Drew, but I have no number for you." There, she hadn't lied and she hadn't given out the number. But Molly felt smug too soon. The woman on the other end of the line was not the type to take no for an answer.

"I know John Stark well enough to know that there is always an emergency number where he can be reached."

"If this is a real emergency, Miss Drew, perhaps I can relay a message."

"Of all the nerve! Wait until I see John about this. I just don't believe it!" By now the once strident voice bordered on hysteria.

"Please understand that I am new to this position and that I feel that it is important to follow J.C.'s instructions to the letter. Perhaps he overlooked your name in telling me who could be given a number, and if so I am sorry, but for right now I must do exactly as I was told."

"You can be sure that he will not be impressed with your loack of common sense when I see him next, Miss Stark." And the receiver on the other end banged down, but could not begin to be as irritating to the ear drum as the voice had been.

Molly wondered if she had done the right thing. Then she decided that the right thing for someone of her short tenure, was to follow instructions to the letter. She'd soon know if that was the best judgement to use. She did hope that this Dian Drew wasn't a frequent visitor to the house, because they obviously didn't like each other at all and hadn't even met. Somehow Molly knew that the person would not be less objectionable to her in the flesh than she was on the phone.

The sun had gone down and dusk was replacing daylight. Molly gathered her towel and the phone and headed back to her room. She took off the amp bikini and slipped on a terry cloth robe. She made a cup of coffee in the kitchen and took that and one of her biscuits, laden with jam, back to her room where she watched television with her eyes while her thoughts were about J.C., and the circumstances at home and the angry Miss Drew. At ten, she turned off the television, took her empty cup back to the kitchen and decided that this day had contained more than enough new experiences and challenges and it was time to go to bed.

The room was warm, so she opened the patie door and let the

soft evening breeze enter the room. She donned a short, thin nightie and laid on top of the covers, delighting in the whisper of cool air over her long bare limbs. She thought that she was so wound up and emotionally spent that sleep would never fome, but it did and she slept so soundly that she never heard J.C. when he entered the house, or her room. She did notice the next morning that her door to the patio was closed and that she had covers over her, but thought she probably didn't remember getting up and closing it herself.

4 CHAPTER FOUR

She had set her alarm for eight, just in case, and was glad she had when it woke her. She showered and put on the wrap skirt, print side out, with a cool white blouse and her sandals and went to the kitchen to make coffee and start breakfast. A simple omelet should do, she decided, with crumbled bacon and fresh mushrooms. There was orange juice in the refrigerator and wheat bread for toast. Her timing was good and he was prompt, so everything was ready and still hot when he entered the kitchen. This was a different J.C. The sun kissed hair was sleep tousled and golden whiskers glittered from his unshaven chin. A knee length blue terry robe was knotted carelessly around him and the blue-gray eyes were slightly hazy, rather than piercing.

"Good morning J.C. I hope you had a good time last night."

He went to the table and sat down, drinking some of the coffee before he was fully seated in the chair. Then he spoke, "Good morning, Molly. Yes, I guess you could say that I enjoyed the party. Were there any calls?"

Molly had forgotten about Dina Drew and their confrontation of the night before, in the bright sunlight of this summer morning, but it all came back in a flash which caused her to flush. "A Miss Drew called."

"Dina? What did she want?"

"She wanted to talk to you. When I wouldn't give her a number she was very upset."

He sat there a moment sipping his coffee and then said, with a slight twitch to the side of his moth, "I'm sure she did. Dina does not accept any obstacle that may be in her path at any time. What did you tell her?'

"Well at first I said I didn't have a number for her, which was true because you specified that it was to be given to only a Mr. Adams. Then she said that she knew you always left an emergency number and she wanted it. I couldn't lie, so I said that if it was an emergency I would relay a message to you."

"I'll bet that met with quite a tirade."

"Yes, it did, and she said you would hear all about my lack of common sense and all when she saw you next. I guess she was implying that her influence would cause me to lose the job."

"I fire incompetents, not people who do as they are told or that don't do as they are told, but use good judgement in particular circumstances. Never have I let someone else judge competence for me."

"I'm not sure if you are approving or disapproving of what I did, then."

"You did fine, Molly. Dina is a very old friend and she does get very possessive sometimes. I know she can be irritating but she does have many good qualities and she is the daughter of my father's oldest and dearest friend. So I make allowances for her bossiness that I would never accept from most other women. Can you understand what I'm saying? I'll handle her onslaught about you when the time comes, knowing your side, and you can rest assured that it will soon be forgotten."

"Thank you," she murmured.

"Now Molly, there is the matter of your bedroom door to the patio being open last night."

"Isn't that all right? It was so warm and I just opened it to get some air"

"I'm going to have the house wired with a security system which did not seem necessary when I bought it. But in the past few months ther have been too many crimes, even in this small area for me to feel as comfortable as I used to, especially when I'm away so much. Until then, when I am not here, I want your door closed and locked when you retire. I know the glass panes could easily be broken for an intruder to gain admittance, but at least the soud of the shatter glass would give you a little warning. The control for the central air conditioning for your room is located right by the door and if you are too warm, please use that instead of the open door, though I realize the fresh air is preferable. I do often sleep with my own door open, but that is on the second story and the overhanging balcony would be difficult to scale."

"All right, J.C., I'll remember." So she hadn't closed her own door or covered herself up either.

When he had finished his breakfast and second cup of coffee, he headed back upstairs to shower and dress and Molly did the cleaning u in the kitchen and then went to make her own bed. J.C.'s laundry from the day before was piled neatly in the laundry room and she would take it up as soon as he came down. She didn't hear his steps on the carpeted stairs, but when he reached the bottom, he called her name.

Molly hurried out of her room into the hall to see what he wanted. "I'll be in my den for a while and then take a dip before dinner. I laid out some clothes on the bed and I'd appreciate your packing them when you go up to make the bed."

"Yes, of course."

"I'll answer the phone if it rings between now and noon so you can tend to what you have to do without being interrupted."

"Fine. I had planned on going down to the market in the shopping center for some fresh berries when I finish your room, if that's all right with you."

"Certainly. I'm really looking forward to that shortcake."

Molly retrieved the laundry and went up to his room. Several aticles of clothing were laid on the foot of the unmade bed and she carefully folded them and placed them in the leather suitcase that was found in the closet. How long did he plan to be ways, she wondered? She had thought in terms of overnight, but he certainly wouldn't be taking this many clothes for so short a stay. When she had finished his room, she picked up the luggage, again admiring the rich leather and initials engraed in script on the gold plate by the handle and thought ruefully how pathetic the case her mother had brought her things in must have looked to him. She knew that he would miss no detail like that.

She set the case by the table at the foot of the stairs and, fetching her purse and keys, went to the garage and the car she was beginning to think of as hers.

Only a few shoppers were in the large store on a Sunday morning and she was in and out in five minutes with the basket of fresh raspberries that she hoped would make a supremely delicious dessert for dinner.

She took the risk of cutting a few flowers for the table and arranged them while the roast was cooking and the potatoes baking. She had been tempted to use the dining room table to serve his Sunday dinner, but he had said that was only for company, so she made the kitchen one look as festive as possible with a lemon yellow spread and the white, yellow and gold flowers arranged in a cobalt blue vase. She used the blue plates that she found behind the dishes that were ordinarily used in the kitchen and took two crystal goblets from the stock in the dining room sideboard.

Again J.C. was very appreciative of her culinary efforts and remarked that the table looked good enough for company. She told herself that all the extra effort and touches were simply because she was so determined to do well and make a success of the job. The tart-sweet fresh raspberries served on the flaky biscuits and topped with billows of sweet whipped cream were even better than she had hoped and when he had finished his, he directed her to serve it for dessert when they next had guests. As they lingered over coffee, he produced two envelopes from the breast pocket of his jacket. "One of these is operating expense money for the house," he said. "I haven't yet had the opportunity to get you charge cards and a checking account for those items so it's cash and should do for a week or so. The other is the list of phone numbers of places I will be and the appropriate times in case you have to reach me. Again, if anyone but Ben Adams calls, you are not to give out the numbers."

"What do I tell Miss Drew?" she asked coyly.

"Dina called while you were out. We had quite a chat. She knows that I'll be away until Wednesday or so, so you should have no problem with her calling."

Molly knew she should keep quiet, but couldn't resist asking, "Did she tell you how terrible I was?'

"Let's just say that I handled her as I usually do and that your job is not in immediate jeopardy from that incident." He stood and she found it necessary to tilt her head back to meet his eyes. "Take care of everything and yourself, Molly. You should be perfectly safe and have phones and neighbors if you need help. You may call me at any of the numbers at any time if you find it necessary."

"I'm sure I'll be quite all right."

"I'll call from time to time to see if there is anything you need to know or if there have been phone messages or the like."

She watched wistfully as he picked up his suitcase and went out to the car and she was still standing by the window as the gray car disappeared from sight over the ridge of the hill

Time seemed very heavy on her hands all of a sudden, and instead of luxuriating in the thought of three or four days with nothing much to do, she suddenly felt very empty and lonesome. She worked slowly at cleaning up the kitchen, but no matter how she lingered over each chore, only an hour had passed when she had to admit that there was not another thing she could do in that room.

She went to J.C.'s den and tried to tidy up the surface of the desk, but she wasn't sure what was important and what wasn't so when she had finished, it really didn't look much different.

She wandered back through the huge quietness of the deserted house. How different it seemed when she was alone in it. She'd call her mother, she decided. It would be good to talk to someone. The phone rang several times but there was no answer. That seemed strange because Sunday afternoons her parents were almost always home. Then she wondered if her father had returned yet. If something serious had happened to him she was sure they would have called, but she began to worry about it.

She tried her home several more times before her sister finally answered the phone.

"Maria, where is everybody? I've been calling all afternoon."

"Sis, Mom is still trying to find Dad. He just doesn't seem to be around town anywhere. She's getting really scared and she may be going to call the police soon."

"Has she tried all his friends and the bars and all?"

"Oh, yes, she did all that last night. No one has seen him since Friday night."

"Where is Mom now?"

"I'm not sure. She went off this morning and said something about a camp or something where he used to go to hunt and fish with some of the guys from work."

"I've heard of it but I have no idea where it is and besides, how would he get there without the car?"

"I suppose he coud have hitched a ride."

"That's possible, but from what I've heard it's pretty remote and I don't like the thought of Mom going there alone."

Maria began to sob, "Oh, Sis, this is such a mess around here since you left and it's only two days. Even Mom is different."

"Calm down, Maria. You will have to start being stronger and more of a help with me not there. She's only upset over dad and when he comes home, she'll be the same old Mom again."

"Will she?" came a sniffling quiery.

"Sure she will. Now listen, Maria. As soon as Mom gets home have her call me and if she doesn't come home by dark, call and I'll see what I can do. Got that?'

"Uh-huh"

"Now in the meantime, start something for supper and use the vacuum or dust or something. You'll fell better if you keep busy and Mom will like coming home to a meal and a tidy house."

"Okay, Sis." Marie said without the usual argument that preceded her doing anything around the house. "Will you tell me your number in case I need to call you?"

Molly gave her the number and thoughtfully replaced the receiver. She got the telephone directory from the front hall table and looked up the number of one of the men that used to be a hunting and fishing buddy of her father's when he was working. She hadn't see him at the house in a couple of years now and din't know if her father was still on friendly terms with him, but if her mother did not return soon, then it would be a place to start. She wrote the number on the notepad by the phone.

It was approaching six now and Molly thought about making something to eat, but although it would be a time filler, the thought of food ahd little appeal. She poured herself a glass of iced tea and sat down at the kitchen table with pencil in hand to plan some menus for later in the week when J.C. would be back.

The shrill ring of the phone shattered the silence of the house and Molly jumped up with her heart in her throat, praying silently that it was her other. It was.

"Oh, Mom, I'm glad you're back. We were so worried."

"I found your father, Molly, but he refused to come home. He's staying in that old cabin that they used to use for hunting and fishing trips and it's iin terrible shape."

"He's all right then?"

"He looks awful and has no food or anything, but I couldn't talk him into coming home, " her mother's voice was choked with sobs.

"Look, Mom, why don't you call a couple of his old buddies. Maybe they can talk some sense into him. And he's bound to come back to civilization when he runs out of liquor."

"I suppose you're right, but what if he wanders off into the woods or falls into the pond when he's drunk?"

"You've done the best you could, Mom, and it was very clever of you to think of that place to look for him, but I wish you hadn't gone way up there alone. Please call some of the men and if you must go back, don't go alone."

"All right, Molly. I'm so sorry that all this had to happen when you were so excited about starting your new job. How is it going?"

"Fine so far. J.C. left this afternoon and won't be back until Wednesday, so I should have lots of time to get used to the house and plan meals and shop and such."

"You're all alone there?"

"Yes, but I'm fine. I don't want to leave tonight as he may call, but I'll stop in tomorrow when I get the shopping done – unless you need me before."

"And you call me if you need any help, Molly, or if anything frightens you."

"Thanks, Mom, I will."

"We'll see you tomorrow then."

"Yes, I'll be there, most likely before noon."

Her mother hung up, almost reluctantly, and Molly realized that she had become her mother's shoulder to lean on since her father had become so unpredictable and unreliable, and that with Molly out of the house, she must feel like a crutch had been yanked out of her hand. A sense of guilt swept over her, but could she be a crutch at home indefinitely? And what if she needed someone to lean on once in a while?

At ten o'clock she went through the house making sure all the doors and windows were securely locked and go ready for bed. Evidently J.C. was not going to call tonight, and why should he? He'd only been gone for several hours and it being Sunday, there wasn't much likelihood of there being business calls. But it sure would be nice to hear his voice, she thought. After her conversations with her mother and sister, an assuring, in control voice would help boost her own confidence and after these several hours of such total quietness, even a call from Dina Drew would be almost welcome to break the monotony.

She got into bed, leaving a lamp on to read by. When the phone rang, it startled her a bit, but she reached for it eagerly

"Hello," she said breathlessly.

"Did I wake you, Molly?"

"No, I am in bed, but I was reading."

"I just got in or I would have called earlier. Everything alright, I trust?"

She wanted to say that it was now, but instead, "Everything here is fine. There were no calls for you."

"Good. Have you heard from you father?"

"Mother found him in a remote cabin that he used to use with some friends as a fishing and hunting camp. He refused to come back with her and she's quite upset. I think she will get some of his old friends to go and help her tomorrow."

"You are not to go."

His voice was one that brooked no argument. Molly was taken by surprise and didn't quite know what to say.

"Molly, did you hear me?"

"Yes, I heard you, but if Mother feels she needs me—"

"You are not to go after him with her. That is a man's job and with his present attitude toward you, I don not think you would accomplish anything except to get hurt yourself."

"Oh, I don't think he'd strike me or anything like that."

"After what I witnessed the other night, I'm not so sure and we both know there are ways to wound that are much worse than physical hurt and that take longer to heal."

"I promised Mom that I would stop by tomorrow after I do some errands in town.."

"you may go to the house if he isn't there and wherever else you'd like to go, except after him."

As much as she appreciated this concern for her well-being, Molly was a naturally independent person, and the hackles on her neck started to rise as she felt resentment start to replace the pleasure she had felt at the sound of his voice.

"I am in your employment, J.C., and I have every intention of carrying out your wishes in that capacity as closely to the letter as I possibly can, but my private life is really my concern."

"It would seem that your private life caused you to take on this job, which I had my doubts about. I shall not interfere with your choice of friends and social activities as long as they don't interfere with your job, but when it comes to your father, I can't help but feel partly responsible for his antagonism toward you and I insist that you do not see him until I get back and am there to face him with you."

She wanted to argue the point, but realized that there was no argument that would sway his decision. Alright. I'll go home tomorrow, but I'll call first and make sure he's not there." His voice softened. "Molly, believe me, this is all for the best. Now go to sleep and I'll call you again tomorrow night. I am expecting some calls tomorrow, but they should be in the morning and you can take the messages and relay them tomorrow night."

"Okay."

He stayed on the line for another few moments, as if he would add something to what he had already said, but he didn't and a soft click told her that he had broken the connection. With a sigh she replaced the receiver and turned out the light. She did a lot of soul searching before falling into a fitful sleep.

5 CHAPTER FIVE

In her dreams, Molly was being pulled in two different directions by two faceless forms, one tall and light and the other short and dark. She was like a rope in a tug of war and utterly helpless to stop either of them, or to make a decision about which one she wished would win. It seemed that no matter which one won, she would still be the loser and she woke up with her mind and spirit feeling heavy and with a vague discontent possessing her.

It was still very early by the clock on the bedside stand, and although she still felt tired, she did not want to return to the world of frustrating dreams, so she walked listlessly out to the kitchen and made coffee. Even the weather reflected her mood, as the heavily overcast sky predicted an impending rain. She made a shopping list while she had her coffee and then decided that a shower and shampoo would make her feel better.

J.C. was not here and she was tempted to crawl into her old jeans and the comfort of her favorite sweatshirt, but thought better of it, and put on the navy skirt with a bright red shirt. Somehow she felt that he would know if she broke a rule without his even being there. Then it dawned on her that this was Monday morning and that in an hour she should be expected to report for work at the salon. In all the trauma of the weekend, she had completely forgotten that she had not notified Isadora of her resignation. She was not in any mood to face that lady today, but knew she must, if Isadora came in today, that is.

A few minutes before eight, she called the salon and was greatly relieved when she recognized Myra's voice on the other end of the line.

"Myra, this is Molly."

"What's up, Molly, are you sick?"

"No, but I'm not coming in. I have another job. Is Isadora around?"

"No, not yet. You know how she is, dropping in unexpectedly or not at all. Hey, what's this other job?"

"You remember the phone call I had on Friday? Well, it all started with that and is just too much to tell on the phone. How about having lunch with me today and I'll tell you about it?"

"Sounds good. I'm off at eleven-thirty. Where shall we meet?"

"I'll pick you up as I have the use of a car. Would you tell Allison that I won't be in and that if and when Isadora comes in, she can call me here or let me know when she will see me?"

"She'll be absolutely livid, you know."

"She should have thought of that Friday when I asked for a raise." Molly gave Myra the number where she could be reached and confirmed their appointment for lunch."

Despite her dread of facing the implacable Isadora, Molly brightened at the thought of having lunch with Myra and sharing her new experiences with that exuberant, but practical girl.

Molly took three calls for J.C. that morning and carefully wrote the messages and numbers down so that she could be accurate in reporting them when he called. She did not hear from her mother or Isaddora, so at quarter past eleven, she rolled out of the drive in the little blue car and headed for the salon.

Promptly at eleven-thirty, Myra came out the door and Molly sounded the horn to let her know where she was. Myra's mouth fell lopen in disbelief when she spotted Molly behind the wheel of the Saab. Then she jogged over, opened the door and got in.

"Hey, if you boss can use any more help, I'm available."

Molly chuckled. "I'm afraid this is a one woman job. I am working as a housekeeper for J.C. Stark and I have the use of the car for shopping and errands and my own activities when he's not using it. He's in Boston until Wednesday, so I have a little time on my own."

Molly drove to a nearby Chinese restaurant that was a favorite of the girls at the salon, because it was inexpensive as well as being cool and pleasant with excellent food. When they were seated in a booth, and had ordered lunch, Myra's lively curiosity could be contained no longer and Moll gave her as complete a rundown of the events that had transpired since she left the salon on Friday as possible.

"Boy, Molly, you have had some weekend." Myra sounded as close to being envious as was possible for her to sound. She was a very generous person and one of the quialities that Molly admired most about her was her genuine pleasure at anyone else's good fortune.

"It's a shame about you dad and all, but this seems like a chance for you to get out and have a life of your own for a change. I was getting worried about you with two jobs and no time to yourself at all."

"Thanks, Myra. But I can't help bet feel a little guilty about my family, even though I did this partly for them."

"You have nothing to feel guilty about and I hope it all works out. I'm sure it will. You're such a worker, Molly, and everyone at the salon loves you. This J.C. person can't help but be pleased with you."

"I hope you're right, Myra, because I'm on trial for a couple of weeks and if it doesn't work out, I don't know what I'll do. I not only won't have a job, but I doubt if my father would let me come back home."

"Don't worry about it. There are always jobs for people like you, even if the money and surroundings aren't as great as what you have now and if you need a place to bunk for a while, our house is a little crowded, but you could share my room until you get on your feet."

Molly's gold flecked brown eyes showed her appreciation as the met the almost black ones in the elfin face across from here.

"Thanks, Myra, I really will miss working with you and seeing you every day. Let's keep in close touch. In fact, why don't you come up to the house tonight and keep me company?"

"Great. I'm dying to see this palace you live in now, Cinderella."

Molly gave her directions to get to the house and they reluctantly left as Myra had to return to work, neither having done justice to the lunch they had ordered.

The platinum Cadillac was parked outside the salon when they returned, and Molly groaned, "Well, I guess my reprieve is over.

Time to face the music."

"You aren't going to let her get the best of you, Molly! You're holding all the cards now. Do a good job."

The entered the coolness of the air conditioned salon which felt overly chilly to their rested bodies. Myra made a circle with her thumb and index finger and Molly smiled ruefully as she headed for the office door.

Friday she would have been delighted to make the announcement that she was about to make, but today she felt a little less brave. Then she thought about the routine she had been following for so long, with another job to face at the end of a long day here, and she squared her shoulders and thought. "J.C., you'll be proud of me," and she entered the lion's den.

Isadora was on the phone and waved her to a chair in front of the cluttered desk. She didn't interrupt her conversation on the phone a syllable, but kept her eyes on Molly the whole time, as if she could destroy some of the armor while she was made to wait. When at long last she hung up the phone, she kept her steady gaze on Molly. "Allison said you were ill today. You don't look ill now."

"No, I am not ill, nor was I this morning. I called to say I wouldn't be in, not that I was ill."

"But Molly, surely you know that is the only legitimate excuse for not coming to work, unless there was a death in the family, perhaps?"

Molly shook her head. "No one died. As you know, Isadora, I need to make more money than you fell you can pay, and an unusual job situation arose over the weekend, one that required my immediate presence. I know that it is usual to give a notice when leaving a position, but this opportunity was too good to pass up, especially when you had only just made it quite clear that there would be no raises in the near future here."

Isadora's blank expression did not waiver, but an unpleasant glint appeared in her eyes. "You do realize that you have left me shorthanded at a very inopportune time, don't you?"

"Yes, and I'm sorry to inconvenience you. I'm sure you can find a satisfactory replacement in a short time, however, and I must think of my future and my family's welfare first."

"That seems to be the prevailing attitude with the modern generation, I'm afraid. Whatever happened to the old work ethic?"

Molly bristled slightly, but tried to emulate the calmness of the woman across from her. "I have worked very hard, especially this past year, Isadora. Not only here, but at another job too. I don't mind work, but I think I do deserve fair compensation for it. You are an excellent business woman, I am sure, and you have been very successful. But I would keep in mind, that a lot of your success is dependent on the girls who work for you and keep the customers coming back. It might serve you well to pay them a little better, before you lose them."

Molly rose and walked to the door, opened it and strode out without a backward glance, fully satisfied that J.C. would have approved of her handling of the situation.

She aimed the car in the direction of her parents' house and decided that since she had done so well with Isadora, she could handle whatever she found there with equal calmness and practicality.

Maria met her at the door, like she had been anxiously awaiting her arrival. She came out on the porch with her finger held to her lips in caution, and takin Molly's arm pulled her back down the steps and around to the side of the house.

Heeding the quiet signal, Molly almost whispered, "What is it, Maria? What's wrong?"

Maria's usually full bodied voice was husky as she tried to keep it low. "He's back, Molly. Some guys went and got Dad this morning and brought him back. Mom put him to bed, but we don't know when he might wake up and Mom doesn't want him to see you right now."

Then Molly remembered that she had told J.C. she wouldn't go near the house if her father was at home and wished, too late, that she had remembered to call first.

"Okay, Maria, I understand. I'll go right now before he wakes up. Tell Mom that I'll call her when I get home. No, it's better if she calls me, then the phone ringing won't wake him or anything. Please keep me posted on what's happening."

Maria nodded mutely and tears threatened to overflow from the liquid brown eyes. There were lots of comforting tings that Molly would have liked to have said to her sister, but she just patted her arm and hurried back to the car. Her mother was standing in the upstairs bedroom window, the room her parents shared, and she did the best she could to put a reassuring smile on her face as she threw a hasty kiss inn that direction and then backed the car out into the street as quietly as possible. She didn't even close the door tightly until she was a way up the street as she didn't want to chance the noise waking her father.

The realization struck her as she pulled up to the big white house that this was the only home she had now. She thought of two famous quotations – "Home is where the heart is." And "You can't go home again," and knew that for her the latter was true already, but what of the former?

She put away the supplies that she had picked up and wished that it were sunny out so that she could swim off some of her tension and start getting a tan on her very white skin. She did need some exercise and fresh air and she guessed the nest best thing was a walk. She changed to her old jeans and sweatshirt, remembered the portable phone, and spent an hour expoloring the lovely grounds that surrounded the house. A grove of maples beyond the manicured back lawn was dark and gloomy on this overcast day, but she knew they would be a pleasant retreat when the sun was out and decided that this would be her "private" spot when she needed to think and get away from it all. She could picture herself among the trees with a carpet of leaves in the fall and a blaze of color over her head to look up at. The she cautioned herself not to make plans too far in advance. She wandered through the trees around to the front of the grounds and emerging from the spruces at the end of the driveway, was astounded to see a car parked in front of the house, the vivid red of it, standing out against the stark white of the building.

Wondering who it could possibly be, she jogged up the drive just as a tall blonde woman turned from the door and headed back toward the sport convertible. She noticed Molly's approach and stood waiting beside the car for her to get closer.

"May I help you?" she panted at the end of the rather long run she had just completed.

The blonde, on closer examination, was almost red haired and Molly found herself confronting a pair of disconcertingly calculating hazel eyes which were thoroughly, but perfectly made up.

"You are Miss Stark, I presume."

There was no doubting the identity of the caller now, not with that voice. Just what she needed, on a day like today had already been, was a face to face meeting with Dina Drew!

"Yes, but won't you call lme Molly? J.C. is out of town for a few days. Can I help in any way?"

"I talked to John yesterday and he said he'd be in Boston this week. I told him I'd drop by and check up on you and the house while he was gone. I thought that would ease his mind with you being so young and inexperienced.

Molly could feel the wave of color rising to engulf her face and know this woman would miss none of it. "Everything is under control. I decided to take a walk and explore the gournds a bit."

"Shouldn't you be on duty? It was my understanding that you had Wednesdays off. What if John got an important call?"

Molly didn't feel that she should have to defend her actions or report her whereabouts to anyone except her boss, but she knew that making more of an enemy than she already was of this woman would not be a good idea, at least not at the present time. "J.C. expects me to do the shopping and visit my family and such, and I have the portable phone right here if anyone should call."

"That man is just too generous with hired help. He doesn't use other than ngood judgement when it comes to business, but I shall have to give him some pointers about running an efficient home." The cool eyes took in the only slightly shorter figure before her and they narrowed slightly as she assessed the lithe figure whose breasts thrust proudly, even against the baggy sweatshirt. Molly know the disreputable jeans would be mentioned to J.C. and wished that she had not changed, but it was too late for might-have-beens now.

"Can I offer you some coffee or tea, Miss Drew? I know that J.C. would expect me to be hospitable to such an old friend of the family."

"No thank you, Miss Stark," and she emphasized the name. "I am working on a very busy schedule today and am not used to passing idle chatter with maids. If John calls, please tell him that I took time to stop in and check and may do so again before the end of the week."

Molly almost told her that he was coming home on Wednesday, but thought better of it. Her face was blazing from the put down, but she thought, I suppose she's used to havin hired help at home and I am not used to being this kind of hired help. So she gulped back the retort she would have liked to thow out and said in seet tones, "I am sure that J.C. will be glad to see you when he gets back. You can be sure I will tell him that you were here."

Dina Drew started the engine and drove off in the same flamboyant manner that she talked—self confidence and an air of authority oozing from every pore.

Molly went slowly into the house which seemed even more deserted than before in the gloom of the late afternoon. Thank goodness Myra was coming up this evening and she would have not only some cheerful company, but an understanding ear to vent her anger on.

When Myra putted up the drive in her brother's old red Subaru, Molly had the front door open before she could come to a stop.

"Gee," Myra enthused, "this is some place. Is it all right to leave this rattle trap parked here or should I hide it somewhere out of sight?"

Molly laughed. "It's all right there. No one will be coming and there's no road by for anyone to see it."

They went into the house with Myra trying to take in everything at once. Molly suggested that they start with the kitchen and then go through the whole house so that she could really enjoy it. When they had completed the tour and Myra had seen every room, bath and closet, they went back to the kitchen for the coffee and snack that Molly had prepared.

"Gee, Molly, this is a super house. Is your boss super, too?"

The question caught Molly by surprise and she didn't quite know what to say. She took another sip of coffee and toyed with the idea of letting Myra in on the thoughts and feelings she was beginning to develop for the man who was her boss, but she wasn't quite sure herself what they were, so she said, "He's a very handsome man and very successful, as you can see by these surroundings. He's most generous with money and so far seems quite reasonable to work for. I really don't know much about him in such a short time."

"Is he young or old or what?"

"I really don't know his age, Myra. I would think maybe he's in his thirties. Surely he must be to be so successful."

"You mean he might be younger?"

"He's certainly not older."

"Wow, you really did find a super job!"

The pixie faced girl interrupted, "I doon't think anything, Molly I'm sure you know hwat you're doing and I wish you all the best.

I'm juust a little envious to think about you working for a young, rich, handsome man while I work for the Dragon Lady."

"You don't have an envious bone in your body and I'm envious of that."

The girls chatted happily until nine and Molly felt quite a bit begtter about everything, including Dian Drew, when Myra got through bolstering her morale. Then Myra announced that girls who put fat ladies through their paces all lday ling, had to get to bed early, and, with a promise to call or come soon, she hopped into the battered little car and rattled off down the drive.

Molly picked up the dishes they had dirtied and decided to curl up in the recliner in J.C.'s inner sanctum to await his call. She was going to turn on the television set, when she thought better of it and picked up a photo album from the glassed in shelves she had notived before. She felt much cozier and less alone snuggled up in the enormous recliner that smelled vaguely of the same after shave that J.C. used. The pictures meant little without any identification, but she assumed that most were his relatives and some must be of him when he was a child. Near the end of the album there were several pictures of J.C. and another, equally tall and handsome man and the loveliest girl she had ever seen. They were captured on film in a variety of poses and settings, in swim suits near a beach, in ski clothes with mountains in the background and in scuba gear. The girl was always in the middle, between the two men, and it would be hard to tell lwhich one she was with. Even in these samlol snapshots, she appeared flawless with long, wavy hair, a gorgeous smile and a perfect figure and legs. Molly knew instinctively that this girl's name was Joan. She snapped the album shit with a bang and put it back on the shelf where she had found it. She almost wished that she hadn't touched it, like it was private and not for her eyes, and she felt a twinge of guilt when she ansered the ring that she knew would be J.C.

"Everything all right up there, Molly?"

"I have some phone messages. Oh dear, they're at the other phone." Molly was as flustered, all lof a sudden, as she would have been had J.C. walked through the door and found her curled up in his special chair going through his pictures.

"No rus and it's only a few steps to the other phone."

A few giant steps she thought. Of course he must have assumed that she answered from her room and only had to step out into the hall. Thank goodness for the portable phone. With that in had, she quickly darted through the den and living room and retrieved the phone pad from the hall table. She gave him the messages and he repeated some names and numbers to make sure that he had them correct.

"Now what else has happened today, Molly? Is you father back yet?"

"Yes, he's back."

"You haven't see him, of course."

"No, I haven't seen him." There was silence on the other end of the connection and she wondered if she were somehow transmitting her uneasiness over the line to him.

"Molly, I sense that something is wrong. Please be honestg with me." His voice was the same familiar firm one, but with a touch of pleading that broke down anyh desire she had to hedge.

"J.C., I've had quite a day and I don't think you want to take the time to listen to all the little details. Everything is under control now, and when you get bavck I'll ltell you all about it."

"That is the most unsatisfactory thing you could have said, Molly, and if you think I'm going to wonder and worry for two more days, you've got another thing coming. Out with everthing!"

The pleading tone was gone now, replaced with a determination that was not to be denied.

Still using the portable phone, Molly went into her room and sank into the chair by the door. She took a deep breath and told him the whole story of her day, from the phone call to Maria, through her exchange with Isadora, the trip to the house and, lastly, of her first meeting with Dina Drew.

"It does sound like you've had quite a day. It bothers me a lot that you went to the house without knowing if your father was home. You did promise me that you wouldn't."

"I know, and I really didn't mean to. I never dreamed that he'd be there. I'll be more careful from now on, I promise, and one other thing..."

"Yes?"

"You might as well hear it from me before she tells you. When Miss Drew came today I was walking outside in the woods and, even though I know you don't approve, I was wearing jeans."

There was a long pause and then she heard what sounded like a smothered laugh but when he spoke it was quite seriously.

"I think that a walk in the woods would be sufficient excuse to wear jeans and quite justified actually."

"Thank you for understanding."

"I try to understand, Molly, in everything that I do. Try to remember that."

"Yes, I will."

"Now are there any other problems or confessions that you would care to cast on this sympathetic ear?"

"Well, I did invite a friend up here this evening to keep me company and show the house to."

His reply was quick and sharp, "A friend?"

"Yes, Myra from the salon. She's my best friend and knows all about my family problems and all and she's great to visit with when you need someone to talk to. You don't mind do you?"

"It seems, Molly, that there are lots of little things that you and I need to sit down and iron out when I get home. I don't mind that you friend came to visit you. I'm sure you are quite lonesome bieing away from your own house and all alone there, but you are not to invite just anyone at any time."

"Oh, I wouldn't do that. When you're here and I'm working I wouldn't think of it."

"That's not exactly what I meant. I'll explain further when I get back. In the meantime, no men friends, please."

Molly was glad that he couldn't see the flush that his remark prompted. "You don't have to worry. I have no men friends," she retorted.

"I find that hard to believe, but as I said, we will discuss it when I get home. Until tomorrow the, " and he hung up.

How could he be so agreeable one minute and so disagreeable the next? Molly returned the phone back to his private room and shut out the lights on her way back to her own room.

That night, the tall light figure in her dream still didn't have a face, but he did have piercing gray-blue eyes and every time she looked at them, she had to turn away or be blinded. The short dark form wasn't there at all. She knew who had won the tug of war. What would he do with the prize now that he had won it? Anticipation, anxiety and a mixture of fear and delight overtook her and she woke with her heart pounding and a sense of confusion that dominated all the other cares she had on her mind. She felt like crying, but she didn't know what about. Though it was still very early, she put on her bikini and stepped out into the chilly morning and dove into the chillier water. She swam until she ws out of breath and out of the clutches of the dream figure who had left his imprint on her waking hours as well as her dream world.

6 CHAPTER SIX

Her mother called later that morning to say that her father had agreed to see a doctor and although she was worried about what he discovered, she was very optimistic that he might now seek treatment to help him with the drinking problem. Molly had her doubts, but kept them to herself and encouraged her mother to keep her spirits up and hope for the best.

She took advantage of the time she had by making and freezing some dishes so that she would have food ready in case of emergency or if J.C. sprung some unexpected company on her. The she took the phone outside and basked in the sun for an hour or so, being careful not to get burned with her skin so unused to the rays of the hot July sun. There were no calls to interrupt her solitude and she found herself thinking more and more of J.C.'s homecoming on the next day. Now that it was only a day away, she felt lighter hearted and less lonely, and she told herself that it was because being in the house alone was lonely and that with him home, there would be more to do to keep her busy.

When she had absorbed all the sun she felt was prudent, she went inside and carefully dusted the still immaculate living room, dining room and his bedroom. She lingered there a while, feeling slightly guilty as she found herself picturing his long, strong body stretched out in the enormous bed with his tousled head on the pillow. She knew he didn't sleep in pajamas, because there was no evidence of any when she tidied his room, and he left all his other garments wherever they happened to land. She had already noticed the brands of toilet items that he used and she checked the stock in the bathroom cabinet to be sure that none needed replacing. She was almost disappointed that there was no excuse to make a trip to the store to buy some.

She laundered all the clothes she had worn and made herself a light supper, after which she went to her room and settled down with a book she had found in the wall unit of her room. The previous occupant must have enjoyed romance novels, as there was a shelf full of the, and she had chosen one with an historical setting.

At nine she started to listen for the phone to ring. At ten she was sure that he would call any minute. When eleven o'clock came and he still hadn't called, she put her book down with a sigh of disappointment and go ready for bed, still hoping that the stubbornly silent phone would break the quietness of the still house.

She didn't know what time she drifted off, but she woke with a start. It wasn't the dream this time, but a lingering sense of a half-heard sound that was not an ordinary night noise. She lay very still with her head pressed against her pillow, straining hard to hear above the loud thudding of her heart. The fear, near panic, overtook her as a crack of light appeared in the doorway. The narrow shaft of light widened and then was partially blocked by a huge, dark shape. She tried to think rationally what her best course of action should be, but her mind just wouldn't function. Then she heard her name spoken softly and the panic that was engulfing her turned to relief. She leaped from the bed and uttered breathlessly, "J.C.?"

She didn't know how she came to be held tightly against him, only that it was such a comforting feeling, with her body trying to recover from the fear that had consumed it a moment ago. A strong hand smoothed her hair as it pulled her head against his shoulder. His body was warm and solid to cling to.

"Molly, I'm sorry I frightened you."

Her relief expressed itself in tears and for a minute she couldn't speak at all. He held her tightly and stroked her head and back soothingly until she was able to control her voice.

"I'm sorry. I was so sound asleep. Then I woke up and saw the door opening, I panicked."

"It's alright, Molly. I decided that I had tended to all the things I need to do and would head right home when I finished. There wasn't any place open along the way to eat or phone from at this time of night, or I should say morning. I didn't want you to hear me prowling around the house, so I decided to wake you by knocking on your door. I rapped several times and got no response."

"That must be what woke me, except I didn't know what it was."

The fear had subsided from her body and her mind was clearing. She became conscious of her barely clad body pressed so closely against his. His arm was still holding her firmly against his thighs and chest and it was far from unpleasant. She was glad that the darkness of the room did not permit him to see the redness that she knew was seeping over her face. She feared that he could feel the heat that was engulfing her body.

"I'm alright now, J.C."

"Are you sure?" He seemed reluctant to loosen his hold.

"Yes, really, I'll make some coffee and fix you something to eat."

"There's no need. I didn't wake you up for that. I can do it myself.

No, I couldn't go back to sleep right now, anyway, and I think I could use a cup of coffee myself."

"If you're sure then."

His arm tightened almost imperceptibly and then he slowly eased his hold and she stepped back, breaking contact with his body. She fumbled in the darkness for her robe. He went toward the door and the overhead fixture flooded the room with light. Her startled eyes blinked as they met his. She knew that he missed no detail of her body which was only lightly veiled by the short, sheer nightie she wore. She froze for a second and then quickly grabbed the elusive robe and wrapped it about her. With head bent, she walked past him and into the kitchen.

As she busied herself with the coffee maker and took out bread and meat for a sandwich, he questioned her about calls, her father and even asked if Dina had visited her again. She answered in as few words as possible, not at all like her usual self.

When the blue and yellow mugs had been filled and he had a thick roast beef sandwich before him, she sat down at the table across from him and took a long drink of the scalding coffee. It burned her tongue and throat, but brought her out of the trance-like state that she had been in. She smiled tentatively.

"I'm glad you're back, despite the fight you gave me."

"I thought it was a pretty nice welcome home," he grinned.

"I'm not usually a fraidy cat. It just was so unexpected."

"Forget it, Molly."

She would never forget it, she was sure. She wondered if he meant the spectacle she had made of herself or that he had seen her almost nude. She didn't expect to ever have an answer to that.

When he had finished eating, he lingered over another cup of coffee. She excused herself to go back to bed. She was becoming more and more uncomfortable in his presence and knew that it was more her own state of mind than anything he had said or done.

"Of course, Molly. Go back to bed and get some sleep. Tomorrow will be a busy one for you as I plan to have three or four people in for dinner. He looked at his watch and noted ruefully that it was after two and that he had better get to bed also.

"I'll clean up the dishes in the morning, if that's all right with you?"

"Sure. And, Molly, I'll be down for breakfast at eight. If I'm not, please wake me up. Don't make anything elaborate. After this middle of the night binge, I'll only need coffee and toast."

"Good night then."

She expected him to echo her remark, but instead he stood and walked her back to her room. As she was about to enter, his hand caught her shoulder and he turned her around to face him. "I'm really sorry about frightening you, Molly. I probably should have chanced that I wouldn't wake you, but I did want to make sure that you were all right."

She raised her head and met his eyes. "It's all right, J.C. I'm glad that you did wake me up."

"Do you really mean that?"

She nodded, her eyes still held by his. The few seconds that he stood there, still holding her gaze with his, seemed like an eternity., but Molly was powerless to break their magnetic contact. Then he smiled and said, "Good night, Molly Stark. Sleep tight." He turned and went back to the kitchen, she presumed to turn out the lights. "She went back to bed.

She slept fitfully, the coffee, her fright and the disturbing exchanges with J.C. all contributed to a less than restful night.

At seven she got up, a little heavy headed, but with a lighter heart than she had had in a long time. She put on the white pleated skirt and turquoise top that accented the touch of color she had managed to acquire in the sun the day before. As she dressed, she planned what she needed to do to have a creditable dinner ready for guests that evening. She wondered if Dina Drew would be among them. Then she frowned slightly at the thought of the woman that she knew had a place in his life, and obviously and important one, Joan.

She pulled the cinnamon rolls out of the oven at exactly eight o'clock, but there was still no sign of the usually prompt J.C. After waiting another five minutes, hoping that he would appear, she went to the foot of the staircase and called tentatively. There was no reply. Slowly she climbed the stairs, one at a time, stopping on every other step to listen for any sound of his stirring. When she had reached the top and he had not answered her call, she went to his door and knocked lightly, expecting an immediate reply. Nothing. She knocked louder and still got no response. Cautiously she turned the knob and opened the door a crack, half fearing that his piercing eyes would meet hers in mockery or anger. He had drawn the drapes and the room was in semi-darkness. She could see the long form stretched out in the bed and could hear his deep even breathing. She spoke his name several times and he turned from his side over onto his back. He still didn't speak or open his eyes. She steeled herself and walked over to the bed, extending her hand gingerly to his bare shoulder and said his name again.

Slowly the eyes opened. It was a moment before they focused on her.

"J.C., it's after eight. You said to wake you if you weren't down by then."

His sleepy eyes held hers. "Mhmm," he mumbled.

"Breakfast is ready."

"Mhmm." He just laid there and stared at her and she didn't quite know what to do.

"You are getting up?"

His eyes still held hers, but the drowsiness had been replaced with a gleam. Then he said, almost angrily, "Yes, damn it, I'm getting up. But I really don't want to and if you don't get the hell out of here right now, I may change my mind!"

His quick change of mood caught Molly off guard and she fairly flew to the door and down the stairs with burning face and pounding pulse. This was a J.C. she had not seen before and she was bewildered and upset. She poured his coffee and put the warm fragrant rolls on the table.

He entered the room almost immediately, clad in the terry robe and, she figured, not much else. He sat down at the table and surveyed the rolls and coffee, then turned to look at Molly. "Where's yours?"

"I had coffee when I got up."

"Well have some more. I need to talk to you about

arrangements for tonight and you might as well join me."

She wanted to protest, but remembered what he had said about arguing about everything, so she filled the yellow mug and sat down opposite him.. She waited while he ate and drank and organized his thoughts. Finally he spoke. "I plan to have three guests for dinner tonight, but it may change to four. It depends on whether Tim is back from San Francisco yet. I realized after I arranged it that I had told you you could have Wednesdays off. I hope it won't disturb your plans any."

"I had no plans so it's all right. I've just started the job and with you being gone, I haven't had much to do."

He nodded. "We'll see that you have another day off in its place. How about Sunday?"

"That would be fine."

"I'll leave it to your judgement what to serve. You seem to be an excellent cook and I guess that you can handle that end. They should be arriving between six and six-thirty. I'll take care of serving drinks and you provide the hors d'oervres. Dinner will be at seven."

"That's fine. Do you have any particular requests about seating or what to use for table setting?"

"I always sit at the head, and tonight, no one will be acting as hostess, so set the other three or four on the sides. You may use whatever you find in the dining room that suits your fancy."

"Thank you. Will you be here for lunch?"

He glanced at the thin gold watch. "With this late start, I'll just grab a bite downtown. I had hoped that we could take care of a lot of loose ends today, Molly, but that will have to wait until later tonight or tomorrow."

He got up and went to the door. He paused a moment, then turned and said, "By the way, Molly, if you ever have to wake me up again, it might be safer for you to throw cold water and run." He grinned and went upstairs.

Molly's heart was suddenly light again. She looked forward to the day ahead of her with so much to keep her busy. J.C. was back and would be coming home tonight, trusting her to do a good job of entertaining his guests. She would show him that she could not only do the job, but be a credit to him.

The fact that she had planned several menus in advance, made it easy to get organized. She cleared the table, started the roll dough rising and made a shopping list, even remembering his request for the raspberry shortcake.

J.C. breezed through the kitchen on his way to the garage, freshly shaved and immaculate in his three piece tan suit and she smiled warmly at his "See you tonight."

As soon as he was out of the yard, she skipped up to his room and tidied the bathroom and made his bed. As she plumped the pillows and smoothed the sheets, she relived this morning's encounter, word for word, and look for look. The realization slowly came that his anger this morning was not because he had woken in a bad mood or that he was cross at having overslept. The remark at the kitchen door, seemingly in jest, was a warning. She was in a sort of paradise, but dangers lurked even there. She must be very careful.

By mid-afternoon Molly had completed everything that could possibly be done ahead of time. She treated herself to a dip in the pool and short bask in the sun. As she entered the house, she heard the doorbell ringing, and still in her bikini and robe, she hurried to the front door.

There stood Dina Drew in an impeccable white linen suit with jade green silk blouse. Not a hair was out of place, despite the top being down on her convertible. And there was Molly, hair still wet, barefoot and wearing a faded terrycloth robe over a very brief bathing suit.

"Miss Stark, you seem unprepared for visitors."

"I took a quick dip as I had all the preparations made for dinner. Will you come in?"

Molly stood aside and Dina swept into the hall surveying everything, missing nothing. "I told John that I would stop in and check out your plans for tonight. I know this is the first dinner party you've handled and I don't want John to be embarrassed."

"I'm quite sure that he will not be. What do you want to check?" Molly drew herself to her full five feet six in her bare feet, but could not equal the presence of the slightly taller woman who was wearing very high heels.

"Well, the menu for one thing and the table setting."

"You will find the menu on the kitchen counter. The table is all set except for the flowers which I will pick and arrange in about an hour so they will be fresh." Now if you will excuse me, I will dress. I'll be in my room if you need any more information." Molly turned and disappeared into the doorway behind the staircase.

Dina stood for a moment looking after the retreating form, then frowned and went into the kitchen. About ten minutes later she knocked on Molly's door. Molly turned off the hair dryer, set down her brush and opened it.

Without any preliminaries, Dina Drew stated her findings. "The menu isn't bad for a beginner, except the dessert sounds quite heavy and unimaginative. The table is fine, except that I have moved one place setting to the foot of the table. I quite often act as John's hostess and I am sure that he intends that I shall tonight."

Molly was about to tell her that those were the only two specific directions that J. C. Had given her about the dinner, but decided to handle it more subtly. "Thank you Miss Drew. I hope that you will enjoy your dinner tonight. Now if that's all, I really need to dress and finish the last minute details."

Dena seemed a little stunned at being dismissed instead of doing the dismissing, but remained for once speechless, and turning on her very high heels, showed herself out. When Molly heard the gears of the fast-moving sports car grinding protest as she sped down the driveway, she smiled to herself and turned the dryer back on.

When JC drove in a little past five, Molly had every detail under control, even to having put the place setting on the dining room table back in its original position. She and I went to with me feel like the government overhead.

He put the car in the garage, so she knew he would be coming in the door. She had a tall glass of iced tea poured and as he came through the doorway, he held it out. He smiled and surveyed her as drank thirstily.

"I was having some things on, this hit. I guess I can wait for my guests get out the boot. You look great in that breaths, Molly. I knew you would."

"Thank you. Did Miss Drew report that everything was all set for tonight?"

"Dena? No, I haven't seen her."

"She came over this afternoon to make sure that I wouldn't embarrass you tonight. She approved of all my arrangements step two."

"Oh?"

"The dessert and the table setting. She thought the shortcake was too heavy and that she should sit in the hostess's spot."

"And you acted on her suggestions?"

"I always follow my bosses orders to the letter." She flushed remembering the phone call she hadn't made in the genes and added, "well, almost always. So I left the dessert as it was planned and changed the table setting back to where it was originally."

"Dena really means well, Molly. She does get carried away sometimes, I hope you will understand and make allowances."

"She obviously would like to be in charge of this household."

"She has a lovely old home that she runs for her father. This one is nothing in comparison to it in size or elegance. I really don't think she finds this house impressive at all."

"Perhaps it's not the house, but the owner that she has her eyes on." The moment it was out, she shouldn't have said it. She looked really distressed as she started to apologize, that he interrupted her with, "Molly, do a good job run running my house, but stay out of my private life." He put down his glass and strode out of the room.

The doorbell rang a little after six and Molly heard J.C. greeting guests in the hallway. She hurried out of the kitchen to take any raps they might wish to have put in the closet. JC introduced her to the couple that had just entered. They appeared to be about JC's age and were very sociable and pleasant, not at all condescending in attitude as Dena was.

Marsha Eli was round faced and a little on the plump side with short dark hair and a wide generous grin. She reminded Molly a little of Myra and she took an instant liking to her. Steve was tall but well short of JC's height. His sandy hair tended to curl and looked like he had struggled vainly to straighten it. His shoulders were very broad and his thick, square neck advertised his former football playing days.

"We were almost forced to cancel due to a lack of a babysitter," Marsha said. "But my aunt agreed to come over at the last minute."

JC turned to Molly. "The Eli's have twins and they are quite a pair. You'll have to see them some time."

"That must keep you very busy. How old are they?"

Marsha made a rueful face. They just turned two and, believe me, when they say terrible twos, they know what they're talking about. And I've got it double."

"And you wouldn't have it any other way," laughed at her husband."

She laughed. "He's right, of course. But it is good to get away for a few hours now and then and have adult conversation for a change."

JC took his guests into the living room and Molly went to the kitchen for the training of hors d'oeuvres that she had waiting. On her way back, Dena arrived and Molly opened the door for her. "Please come in, Miss Drew. JC and the other guests are in the living room. Won't you join them?"

The smile that Dena had pasted on her face in anticipation of JC's opening the door, froze and then turned to a half pout. "I must say that it is on staff, start. Would you please tell John that I would like to talk for a moment in private before I join the others?"

Molly realized that although the words were phrased as a question, they were, in actuality, a command. Hiding her resentment with a cool, "of course, miss Drew," she went back to the living room. JC was mixing drinks at the marble top table he had set up as a bar. She said, as quietly as she could, "Miss Drew would like to speak to you alone for a moment."

He looked up and she caught the flicker of a strange look in his eyes before he answered her. "Would you serve these two Marsha and Steve, please, and tell them that I will be back shortly?"

She nodded and he strode purposefully from the room. She served the drinks and asked if there was anything she could do to make them more comfortable. They were curious about some objects on the mantle and she wished she had the knowledge to answer their questions. JC was gone longer than she anticipated and, she was sure, longer than he had planned. The Eli's caps chatting with her and she found their company enjoyable and not on a servant – guest level.

When the doorbell rang, he thought that AC would be in the hall and answer, but on the second ring, it appeared he would have to. She excused herself and hurried to the door.

A young man with black hair and dancing blue eyes stood there. When he saw Molly, his mouth broke into a wide grin and he said, "I'm Tim Murphy and I hope that you are my surprise dinner partner for the evening."

Molly couldn't help but grin back. He had the most disarming smile that she had ever encountered. It made him look more like a little boy than the adult that he was. "I'm afraid not, Mr. Murphy.

I'm JC's housekeeper. My name is Molly. Won't you come in and join the other guests. JC will be right with you I'm sure."

"Molly, and I'll bet your Irish too."

"I don't think so. Mostly English I think with touches of lots of other things. We just call ourselves Yankees."

"Molly what?"

She had hoped that the question would not be asked, but she sighed and got ready for the usual questions that she encountered when people found out her last name was the same as that of her employer.

"Molly Stark."

"You are related to John are you?"

"No, she isn't."

Molly had been unaware that JC was in the hall. He must have come down the stairs when she was engrossed in conversation with Tim Murphy.

Campus grin narrowed a trace at JC's curt reply, but he stepped forward and that is and out in the two men ends warmly. "You can't blame me for being curious, John. She certainly is young and beautiful be a housekeeper. I thought that maybe while I was away you had succumbed to the bonds of matrimony."

"No, Molly is new in my employ. She is very young for the job. She's still on trial, but seems to be handling everything efficiently."

"If you decide you don't want her, she can always come to my house."

Molly was embarrassed at being discussed as if she wasn't even there and she could feel the prickles in the back of her neck that meant she'd better make a quick exit or she might say something that she would regret later on.

She hurried into the kitchen and checked all the pots on the stove. She arranged the first course on a tray ready to take the dining room soon as they were ready. Dena had not reappeared with JC and she wondered where she was and what they had discussed.

At seven, she went to the living room to see if she could begin serving. She saw that Dena had joined the group and was sitting very close to JC. She seemed subdued and a little pensive. If one looks closely, the eyes looked a little red beneath the perfect makeup, Molly caught JC's eye and he nodded and stood up, announcing that dinner was ready and they could take their drinks to the table with them if they wished.

The food turned out well and she had many compliments on her cooking as she quietly removed the dishes and served each course. JC was usually engaged in conversation and did not comment, but she noticed that his eyes followed her every movement and missed nothing of what she said or did. She was kept on her toes fielding Tim Murphy's frequent remarks to her and she wished that he would cool it a little as she sensed JC's disapproval. Dena was surprisingly quiet and ate little.

When the last dessert was served and the coffee poured, she sat down at the kitchen table and let weariness sweep over her. She was far from finished, but she didn't think she'd have to face the guests again. Coffee with go. She did not want a space fee again morning. That in her present he would not be at her best handling anything.

When the guests had retired to the living room for after dinner drinks, she cleared dining room table and stacked the dishwasher. It would have to go through two cycles to handle all the dishes in pants, so she stacked the rest on the counter until the first was finished. The second load was washing and the first had been put away when she heard JC bidding farewell to the Eli's. Tim left next which left him alone in there with Dena.

When the second load of dishes was done and put away, Molly still had not heard Dena leave. She was dog tired. It was 11 o'clock and she felt perfectly justified in calling it a day. She thought about saying good night or asking if she was needed for anything else, but felt awkward about disturbing them. She didn't know what she might find if she were to walk in unannounced. So she turned off the kitchen lights and went to her room.

She had just climbed into bed when she heard voices in the hall and it appeared that Dena was finally leaving. With in a few minutes she heard his footsteps approaching her door and with a weary sigh, she got out of bed and already had her robe on when he not. She opened the door.

"I want to talk to you, Molly."

She nodded and stood back waiting for him to enter. He stood there a minute looking at her and then said, "let's go into the living room."

He led the way and she followed, clutching her robe tightly about her. Although she was tired, she was very conscious of his powerful body and even more so of the way she was feeling about being alone with him. Only one lamp was burning, that being at the end of one of the sofas. He gestured for her to sit down and she did, while he stood, leaning his arm on the mantle. He looked down at her. Her head rested against the luxuriously soft velvet and hurt Braun up under her. For a moment he said nothing. Then he spoke softly, almost tenderly. "I know you're tired, Molly. You did a super job and I'm proud of you."

"Thank you," she murmured.

"But I can see that no matter how good a job you do, your age and, shall we say, physical attributes, are going to get in the way."

"What do you mean?"

"Dena pointed it out to me and Tim reaffirmed it. Everyone who comes here is going to either assume that I have you here as more than just a housekeeper, or in Tim's case, and send their selves. I am not comfortable with that."

"Does that mean I'm fired?" Molly's voice was flat, almost listless. She had wanted to make him proud of her, had done her best and now she was being ousted wasn't her fault.

"No, Molly, I'm not firing you. I wouldn't be that unfair. I know that I couldn't live with my own conscience if I sent you home right now, and I know that you gave up two jobs to come here. It's been less than a week that I have known you, and you seem to have created more problems in my life than I ever had before."

"I'm sorry. I didn't mean to. I'll leave. Myra said I could live with her if things didn't work out."

"Damn it, Molly, I don't want you to leave."

She looked up in anguish," what do you want, JC? I've tried my best and if that isn't good enough for you then —"

with a muffled oath he strode to the couch and pulled her to her feet. "Do you know what I want right now, Molly? Do you really want to know?" His lips crushed hers so fiercely she could feel the tender flashing grind against her teeth and the steel bands that held her body against him forced all the breath from her body. She was too surprised to struggle or protest and such an effort would have been futile. When she thought she must fade from lack of oxygen, his arms eased a bit in his mouth softened on hers, probing, seeking a response. How she wanted to let him have his, just drift off on a cloud of passion and never look back. But this was not a dream. It was very real and she knew that if she did as her body willed, her pride would have to do the paying in the light of day.

"No, JC, please let me go," she breathed.

"Molly, you want me to, I know you do."

"Not now, not like this. Please, JC I just can't –." Her tears seemed to come from nowhere and herself. Now he really would think of her as an immature schoolgirl and that was the last image of her that she wanted him to have. He put her gently away from him.

"I didn't mean to frighten you, Molly. I guess I thought you were a little more worldly than you are. Go to bed now and we'll straighten things out in the morning."

"No, I don't want to straighten things out in the morning," she sobbed. "I want to straighten them out right now."

"I'm waiting for your suggestions."

Molly wiped her tears on the sleeve of her robe. "Couldn't I work here just days when you're here and stay to watch the house nights when you're gone? I, early in the morning and leave after dinner and then –"

before she could finish, he interrupted her with, "and where would you sleep?"

"At home."

"You are not going back there, Molly."

"Mom said dad agreed to go to the doctor today. If he gets straightened out, then everything would be fine."

"It is a very big word, especially with a drinking problem. No, Molly. That won't do."

"You are responsible for me, you know. I am well and I can take care of myself."

"You are not long over age I am responsible since I got involved the whole situation and, in part, created it, however unintentionally. Now I wish that you would go to bed and let me think."

"I don't think I could sleep."

"And I damn well know that I can't. Put on your suit and will go for a swim in the pool. Maybe that will help clear a couple of heads around here and it's bound to be relaxing."

Molly nodded and went to her room to change. When she stepped through the French door of her room, he was already in the water and she walked to the deep end and dove in. She came up with him beside her.

"Race you to the other end?"

"You're on," she said and struck out in her smooth crawl.

He was taller and stronger and although he made more splash than she did, it was really no contest. They swam side-by-side for several laps of the pool and then climbed out and sat with their feet dangling in the water.

"Feel better?" He asked.

She nodded and then realized that it was too dark for him to see her that well so she spoke, "yes, I feel better."

"You looked like a Goddess coming out of your room in that bikini."

His remark was unexpected and she tensed. He went on, "I was really furious with Tim tonight. I think he really is smitten with you, but he didn't have to be so obvious."

"He seems very nice."

"I usually think so. He's very young. Only a few years older than you are."

"He seemed young and full of high spirits. Is he always like that?"

"He's always good-natured. He likes girls and I presume has more conquests than he can count. I'm sure he'd like to add you to the list."

"Are you saying that he loves them and leaves them?"

"I really don't know that much about his private life, but I'm sure he has his share of affairs, as most young men do now a days."

"Thank you for the warning, but he doesn't seem very dangerous."

"Oh, I'm sure that he uses his charm, not his strengths to make any conquests."

"JC, did Ina have some more bad reports about me?"

"Dena had lots of things to say. Somewhere about you and some more about other things. I was not in the frame of mind to listen tonight and I'm afraid that I laid it on the line to her rather strongly that her interference was not welcome. I'll make it up to her when I see her again later on."

"I'm sorry if I caused any of the problems between you. She just irks me no end and I know I should just be quiet, but it's so hard."

"It's all right, Molly. Mostly it's because she doesn't like the thought of your being here with me. If you were fat, or old or ugly, she wouldn't be half as picky."

"Is she in love with you?"

"Dean is in love with wealth and position and she's getting to the age when her father think she should marry. I just happen to be around and to fit the bill on those qualifications. However, she doesn't fit mine, so I am trying to give her the hand gently that she is wasting her time."

"Who is Joan?"

"My, we are getting personal aren't we? One might think that – no, never mind. Now, Molly Stark, you have two choices. Either you take that gorgeous body inside and lock all the doors, or I will pick you up in my arms and carry you over to that lounge and make love to you."

Polly jumped to her feet, face aflame and fled. She heard his lap ringing out after her and the splashes he dove back in the pool. She really didn't think that he meant what he said about the doors, she locked them anyway.

The tall fair figure of her dreams was faceless no longer and he laughed as she struggled to free herself from his hold.

7 CHAPTER SEVEN

Molly woke the next morning with the ominous feeling that this morning was not going to be easy. JC had made it quite clear last night that things could not go on the way they had been, and she was apprehensive of the decision she feared he had made. She made up her mind that he would not believe or not, having the least flattering outfit on, she went to prepare breakfast.

He was very prompt this morning and already dressed for the day and a conservative suit. She wondered if this was as much his armor for the morning as the need, but flattering, clothing she had chosen to wear herself.

"Good morning, Molly."

"Good morning, JC. Your juice and coffee are ready and I will have your eggs as soon as you tell me how you would like them."

"No eggs. Just some toast this morning, please."

"If you would prefer something else, I can make it."

"No, just toast." His reply was short and she didn't attempt to change his mind. When the toast was ready, she poured herself a cup of coffee and sat down at the table opposite him.

"Will there be any guests for dinner tonight?" She had to break the silence that was hanging like a dark cloud and threatening to undo her nerves altogether.

He met her eyes directly for the first time. "No, no guest tonight. In fact, I will not be here for lunch or dinner."

She hoped that he might elaborate on his remark, but instead silence closed in again. She finished her coffee quickly and taking her empty cup to the sink, rinsed it and put it in the dishwasher. There wasn't much she could do to act busy, since he had had so little breakfast. So she said, "if you don't want anything else, I may as well go upstairs and do your room now." He nodded silently and without another word passing between them, she hurried upstairs.

She heard him drive off a few minutes later and suddenly felt like she was alone in the world and that it was not a very pleasant place to be. She finished the chores and called home. Her mother reported that her father had been admitted to the hospital for a number of tests and they were awaiting the results. She would be at the hospital most of the day. Molly said that she would drop in at the house and make sure that Mike and Maria were all right and see if she could help out at all. She asked if she could visit her father and then remembered what JC had said.

"Probably it's better if you don't right now, Molly," her mother's side. "He is not too happy about being thinking all that I can make him this. Perhaps in a day or two things will be different."

"I understand, mom. But I will go to the house and, since my boss will not be here for lunch or dinner, I'm sure it's all right if I do think is at home to help you out."

"If you're sure all right, Molly, I would really appreciate it. I never realized how much it you were gone, and with your dad taking so much of my time, I'm afraid things in the housekeeping department."

Molly finished the laundry and returned it to AC. Having satisfied herself that there was nothing else she could do make the house look any better, she got into the car and headed for home.

Clouds had moved in and that they had become. He decided that when she got home she would call the salon see if Myra would have lunch with her. That was the best antidote she could think of for her low spirits.

Mike was home and greeted her with enthusiasm. Even before he pointed out M without an argument. They are while they were and Molly listened with half an year's adolescent problems. He seemed satisfied that she was there and listening to your notice that this was not the end's sister he was used to sharing competences with.

When everything was in the kitchen except the floor, Molly suggested that now would be a good while the lawn. He wasn't thrilled, but he did go out and start mower.

Molly didn't hear the car pull in with the mower going, so when she heard JC speak, she almost dropped the handle of the mop she was using.

"I thought I might find you here when there was no answer at home."

"JC"

"Evidently I don't keep you busy enough."

She flushed. "My dad's in the hospital and mom is spending a lot of time there. You didn't need me today, so I thought I'd help her out a little. We can call this my day off this week if you like."

"That is hardly necessary, but I do wish that you had mentioned it to me this morning, or call the office. I was quite concerned when I tried the house for over an hour and couldn't get you."

"I'm sorry. I never dreamed that you would call. I'll not do it again."

"Well, finish this job up and I'll take you to lunch. He consulted his watch. "There are a couple of calls I need to make from the office. I should be finished in half an hour or so. Can you be ready by then?"

"Yes, it won't take long to finish here."

"Good. Then meet me at the restaurant where we ate Saturday. I think that I found an ideal solution to our dilemma, at least for a while. I'll tell you about it then."

Without further ado, he laughed and Molly finished the kitchen floor and went out to tell Mike that she had to leave.

"Boy, sis, who was that neat guy?"

"That's my boss, Mike."

"Two cars? He must be read as all get out."

"I guess you could say that. You'll have to come to the house someday and see that, if you are impressed with cars." She wondered after she had said it, she was being too premature. She didn't know yet what his plans were for her and maybe they didn't include her staying on.

"That would be neat, sis."

"I'll have to let you know when, Mike. I have to get JC's permission of course."

"Sure. Just let me know."

With some parting instructions about helping their mother,

Molly got back in the car and headed for the restaurant. She wished now that she had worn something more attractive since she was going to be seen with JC in public, but there wasn't time to go home or change.

She was a little early. He had not arrived yet, so she took a booth and ordered coffee, instructing the waitress to come back when her boss had joined her. It wasn't long before his imposing form was coming through the door, and when he spotted her, he strode purposefully in her direction.

"I'm sorry I wasn't here to meet you, Molly."

"I was a little early. The waitress will be here directly. I asked her to watch for you."

They ordered and Molly sat on pins and needles waiting for JC to reveal the "ideal solution." He finally dismissed the waitress and almost smiled. "I think that you will like what I'm going to tell you, Molly. I hope so anyway."

Her eyes begged him not to keep her in suspense any longer.

"This morning I called my grandmother, who lives in California. He is not really in good health, it's more a summer. I suggested that a year for the remainder of and she is quite excited about it. I think her presence in the house there are a lot of problems that seem to have arisen with your being. She is a fine lady and quite active. I think you two would get on very well. He doesn't drive, you could take her wherever she wants to go, when I'm not available."

"It sounds great."

"Of course, it would mean more work for you."

"You know I don't mind that. And it will be nice to have someone else in the house when you're away."

He grinned, "she's quite the conversationalist. You won't be lonesome with her around, I can assure you."

"When is she coming? I'll have to get a room ready and all."

"She's hoping to have everything prepared for early in the week. I expect her to give me her flight schedule by Sunday. She lives in a condominium and will not have many arrangements to make."

"I assume you'll put her in the big room at the other end of the hall from yours?"

"Yes, that will be the best arrangement. It's large, has a great view and will give her a little more privacy than the others. I'll have a television installed up there as she is a soap opera fan, despite all her cultural interests, and if she hasn't changed since I last saw her, likes to watch the old movies on late-night shows."

"She sounds like quite a lady."

"She is, Molly. You may have your hands full trying to keep up with her. Now, what is the report on your father?"

The food arrived and Molly waited until the waitress left the table. She shook her head. "There is no news yet. He's in the hospital and reluctantly undergoing several tests. Mom should have some kind of report soon."

With JC's news of the impending visit of his grandmother, the air between them was cleared considerably and Molly really enjoyed the food. She noticed that JC was eating as if you were famished, which he probably was having eaten no breakfast. They chatted between mouthfuls about arrangements for making his grandmother comfortable and some tentative plans for her entertainment. Molly found herself relaxing and enjoying his company once more. His manner was also more like the JC she had first met and she felt that now everything would be all right. She forgot that they would be alone at the house together for a few more days.

When they had eaten and it was approaching 1 o'clock, he said that he would have to take care of some business that afternoon and needed to start right away. As they parted at the door, he asked, "I think I will be able to get home after all."

"Of course, what time shall I expect you?"

"Well, I'm not sure when I'll finish, seven should be a safe time. If I'm home sooner, then I'll just have to have a swim and a drink first."

She blushed, remembering their midnight swim last night, but she met his eyes and nodded.

On the way home she stopped at a vegetable stand and bought several ears of corn and some small, freshly picked summer squash. She would serve these with the special meatloaf that she had in the freezer and there was plenty of time to make a pie.

In the late afternoon, she went for a swim and added to the golden color that was now making her skin look like honey. When JC arrived at 530 his eyes showed his approval of the light blue knit dress and she almost wished that she had kept on the outfit she had worn earlier. He took his drink outside by the pool and had his dip.

She watched him from the kitchen window, bronze body clad in brief baby trunks, and she felt again the strength of the arms around her, the power of the muscular thighs and the comfort and torment of the broad, golden haired chest. As if he felt her eyes, he looked toward the house and she quickly turned away and set the table.

His dress was casual this evening – tan chino slacks and an open necked knit shirt in beige and white stripes. The dinner she had prepared met with his approval and they discussed further his grandmother's impending visit. He told her what he remembered of that lady's preferences and she made careful mental notes of what she would do with the room.

"By the way, Molly, I forgot to ask you how the household money was holding out? Do you need more right away?"

"Oh, no, there's plenty left. It should do very well for at least another week, I think."

"Well I opened the household account today with your name on it as well as mine. Please take care of the expenses from that account from now on. I shall make the deposits and keep tabs on the balance. You can give me a monthly list of the checks you write. You whine for the right one." He drew a check from his pocket and handed it to her. "These can be used until the printed ones arrive in a week or so."

"Do you want me to take care of the electricity and phone bills and the like?"

"No, the bills that arrived in the mail, I'll still handle for now. This money is for the food, dry cleaning, keeping the laundry and bathroom supplied with soap and the like. If you need help with a party or a caterer or we need linens or whatever, go ahead and get them. Just warned me if the expense is going to be extraordinarily large so that I can be sure there is enough in the account."

"How much is extraordinarily large?"

"Let's say if it will bring the month's total to more than $1000, then let me know."

Molly looked at him in surprise. "That's a lot of money. I expect that I can feed you for a lot less than that!"

"Don't forget that there are a lot more things than just mood to buy, and when I entertain, the liquor and the like can really add up. By the way, when your car needs gas take it to the gas station in the shopping plaza and have it put on my account."

"Thank you."

Molly stood and began to clear the table. JC seemed reluctant to get up and leave the room. He sipped on another cup of coffee and watch her as she moved efficiently and gracefully between the table and the sink. She finished loading the dishwasher and put all the leftovers away, wiped the countertop and stove and finally asked if he minded a little so she could wipe off the table.

"Am I in Your Way, Molly? I didn't realize. I'll get out of here and let you do your work in peace."

"It's all done but the table."

The phone rang and he's. "I'll get it, Molly." When the home week and back into the kitchen. He did not look happy. "It's for you Molly."

"Is it my mother?"

"No, it's not your mother. It's a man's voice and I have my suspicions about who it is, but I'll let you find out for yourself."

Molly went to the hall phone and JC stayed in the kitchen, but she knew that he was in earshot of the conversation.

"Hello," she said.

"Molly, my lass, this is Tim Murphy. We met the other night. I hope you remember me."

"Yes, I remember."

"I have a free evening and although I know it's the last minute, I was wondering if you would care to see a movie with me."

"I can't leave tonight, I'm working."

"You must have some time off."

"Yes, I do, but not until Sunday."

"Would you let me take you on a drive Sunday then? We could go to the beach."

"I'm not sure about it. My father is in the hospital and I may needed at home."

He was not going to be put off easily, and Molly began to think that a day away from here and away from JC might be a good idea.

"I'm in the book, Molly. If you find out that you can go, even if it's not until Sunday morning, call me. I'll be waiting anxiously to hear from you."

"All right, I'll call you one way or another by Sunday at 10."

"You bet! Don't let me down, Molly."

They exchanged goodbyes and she hung up. She went back into the kitchen and picked up the sponge she had left on the table. When she didn't offer any information about the caller, JC spoke. "That was Tim wasn't it?"

"Yes, it was Tim."

"I suppose you think it's none of my business what he wanted."

"Do you think it is?" She didn't look at him, but knew that the blue-gray eyes would have a spark of fire in them.

You are both employees of mine and as such, I am naturally concerned about your welfare, however, I suppose you are quite right when it comes to your social lives, as long as it does not affect either of your performances on the job. Just remember, Molly, that Tim Murphy has an awful lot more experience with women than you obviously have with men."

"Don't worry I can take care of myself."

"Can you, Molly?" JC was close in back of her now and she determinedly went on wiping the immaculate table, refusing to meet his eyes. She tensed as his hands grasped her shoulders. Slowly, but firmly he turned her to face him. "Look at me, Molly."

Painfully she raised her eyes to meet his, feeling like they were probing her very soul. Mutely she nodded. His eyes refused to release hers, even as he lowered his head, until the intensity between them became more than she could bear and they closed just before his mouth came to hers. She braced herself for the onslaught of before, but this time his mouth was gentle, persuasive, totally disarming. Her traitorous lips responded in her body there, melting against his. The kiss was both preventable and all too short. She wanted to be, at last, put her away from him, and with her shoulders still held in his extended arms, all she wanted was to be drawn close again is hard, warm body and lose herself her emotions again. One hand moved to her chin and raised her head, forcing her meet those electric eyes again. "Can you, Molly?" He repeated softly. Then he released her and was gone.

Her body was limp and her mind was in shock. She sank weakly into the chair and tried to pull herself back to normal. Slowly strength returned to her limbs and her senses sharpened. Resentment replaced the languor that had consumed her, and she was almost angry. She would not let him dictate her every movement, her friends and her free time. She would go with Tim on Sunday, she decided, whether he liked it or not.

She did not see JC again that night. She assumed that he was in his den. She retired to her room and spent most of the evening half dreading that he would knock on her door. But when he didn't, she felt disappointed that he hadn't.

In her dreams, she was held at arm's length by the tall, fair figure, her feet just above the ground, while the marketing eyes held hers, but refused to either draw her closer or let her go. She woke with a feeling of is that refused to let her drift back to sleep. It was barely dawn, and she watched the sky turn to pink, then gold. It was only five, but she knew she would sleep no more, so she put on her bikini and went out to the pool. The water felt brisk, then warmer than the air. She swam smoothly, silently as a seal. Her arms began to protest and still she swam until it seemed she couldn't take another stroke. She dragged her spent body from the water and lay gasping for breath on the edge of the pool. She closed her eyes to the rising Sun and slowly her pulse returned to normal and her protesting muscles relaxed.

"I think you'd better dry off and dressed before you catching pneumonia."

His voice shattered the silence of the morning and brought her hazy mind back to reality. She sat up quickly, very conscious of her brief attire, and raised her head in the direction of his voice. He was standing on the balcony outside his room, looking down on her, tall and imposing. The Terry robe was his only attire. Muscular, bare legs supported his very masculine frame. Self-consciously, she stood, wishing that she had brought a towel or robe to cover her body which felt so exposed to his gaze.

"I didn't mean to disturb you. I thought you'd still be asleep."

"You disturbed me all right. Get the coffee on will you? I need some right away."

"Of course. I'll only be a few minutes." She almost ran for the door in her haste to get away from his probing eyes.

She dressed quickly and pulled her wet hair back with a ribbon. She hurried to the kitchen and had just put the coffee on, when he appeared. Her heart pounded. What would his mood be this morning? She prayed he wouldn't take up where he had left off the previous evening. Yet, when he noncommittally sat down at the table, she felt let down.

Finally she broke the awkward silence herself. "Would you like eggs or pancakes or something like that?"

"Just juice and coffee for now, please."

She poured the juice and wished the coffee were already finished. She set the glass down in front of him and quickly went back to the work area of the kitchen, as though her close watching would make the coffee maker work faster. When it was done, she filled the blue and yellow mugs they always used and sat down across from him.

He sipped the hot brew for a few minutes, then looked across at Molly. "I talked with grandmother again on the phone last night. She is an organized lady and she said that she would most likely be flying into Boston by Monday evening. She is very spry and active, but she is in her 70s and I think that it would be too much to bring her here Monday night. A two-hour drive after flying cross country might be quite taxing for her. She'll confirm her plans with me tomorrow night and I expect that I will be meeting her plane at Logan. We'll stay over in my apartment in Boston and come here on Tuesday. That is, unless there is shopping or something that she wants to do first."

"I'll have to get going with her right away then."

"I'm sure that it is fairly comfortable now."

"I had the cleaning lady do it thoroughly yesterday, but I'm sure that there are other charges you would want added, since she will be here a while."

"I mentioned that we will need to add television set for her. I'll arrange for that today. They should be able to deliver it and connect it sometime Monday, Tuesday at the latest. There will own, but we did. I'd like to pick out why. I think that writing table or desk or be welcome as well. She has always kept a close bond with friends all over the world. I have meant to some furniture to the upstairs balcony never gotten around. This would be a good time to do it. I'm sure that she enjoy watching the sunset from there and breathing in some pure air."

"That sounds like a good idea. I'm sure she'll love it. That sort of, and certainly large enough to accommodate television and death."

"Then shall we head out at now? With such an early start this morning you should have plenty of time to get your work done by then. "

"We?"

He looked at her with the piercing gaze she knew so well. "I had assumed that you would help me choose the most appropriate items, since Joan is away right now and unavailable to assist."

"I'm sure that I don't have the decorating qualifications that she has, but if you say so, of course I'll help." Her voice sounded howdy, even to her own years. She resented this Joan person for no reason, other than that she seems so important to JC.

"Then the two of us will do the best that we can without somehow I think we'll do that." He finished his coffee and excused himself.

Molly finished her coffee thinking that she would have to get busy to get everything done, especially if she were to have a free day tomorrow and spend most of today with JC. Perhaps it would only take a couple of hours to find the necessary articles. His decisions were quick and decisive and she could see no reason for them to be otherwise when it came to furniture.

When that kitchen and bedrooms were finished, she started the laundry and had time to do her hair. She changed to the white skirt and her favorite turquoise hop and added a fine gold chain and large turquoise earrings. She was becoming quite tanned, for her, and her hair had acquired a son street look that was flattering.

JC's eyes were unreadable when he entered the kitchen just before the appointed hour of departure, but she thought she saw and went in them. He had removed the golden bubble and the Slack war were the same shade as his eyes, while the white, short sleeve shirt contrasted strongly with the bronze of the golden haired arms.

"I see you're ready, Molly shall we hit the road?"

She preceded him to the garage and slid into the sleek gray car, as he held the door for her. She nostalgically recalled the last time she had ridden in this vehicle with him. Was it only a week ago?

"We will go to the television company first and get that ordered. Then I thought we'd look for the other items more leisurely. I don't want to choose something hastily and then have to watch agony on Joan's face when see sees that I have destroyed her decorating scheme. She did all the bedrooms, except my own, herself and that one is her particular favorite."

"It's a lovely room. The colors are soothing and quite warm

at the same time."

"Those are the colors that she favors and that flatter her. Although, I really don't think she could were anything that would look unattractive. She has the ability to make whatever she wears look good."

Molly had felt attractive in her own attire and had taken pleasure in the fact that she looked particularly nice this morning. Now she found herself remembering the flawless girl in the photo album and she could picture her in the room she had created in her own image. Suddenly she felt dowdy and insignificant in comparison. Had she created the room with her future in mind? Was this the room that she expected the share with JC eventually?

Unthinkingly she replied, "yes, she certainly is one of the most beautiful women I have ever seen."

JC glanced quickly in her direction, before putting his attention back on his driving.

"You've not met Joan?"

Molly could feel the color suffuse her face. Now she really done it. There was nothing she could do but admit that she had taken the liberty of looking at the photo album. She didn't know what his reaction would be. He had every right to be angry at her infringement on his privacy and she steeled herself for the worst.

He didn't say anything for a moment, then, "I'll have to show you the rest of my collection of photos and introduce you to them by name. It must be quite frustrating to look at pictures and only guess who they might be."

"I'm sorry, JC I know that it was impetuous of me, but I was waiting for you to call and there wasn't anything on TV that I cared to watch. Curiosity got the best of me I'm afraid."

"Had I known you were interested, I'd have taken the time to point out some of my family members in the photos on the wall. When we get back I'll do so. I'm sure you will feel more comfortable with grandmother if you've seen her photo before you meet her."

"Thank you. I'd like that very much."

An uneasy silence followed and she was relieved when he pulled the car into a vacant space in front of the television company.

The salesman seemed to recognize JC and assured him that hooking up another set on Monday would be no problem. JC contemplated a large screened floor model and then decided that they would get a table model that could be concealed in an appropriate piece of furniture. He didn't think that the room would be enhanced by console no matter how attractive. Molly nodded in agreement and she chose a remote control set that grandmother could operate from the bed if she chose to.

They visited the several furniture stores and came up empty-handed. JC took his time in each establishment, and each time dismissed whatever they had to offer. At noon, they made no other purchases and Molly was hungry and beginning to feel her lack of restful sleep. As they left the last furniture store in town, he looked down at her, concerned in his eyes.

"Are you all right, Molly? You look quite pale all of the sudden."

"I am a little hungry."

JC glanced at his watch. "Of course you are and so am I. We had no breakfast, to think of it. Our next stop will be lunch and then we can decide where to go from there."

They went to a restaurant that Molly had never visited before, though she had driven by many times. The decor of the Victorian style house, had been kept intact and they were seated in one of several small rooms that was profuse with hanging plants and which featured small tables for seating 2 to 4 people. Their table was by a window and looked out over a rock garden. JC ordered wine for both of them without consulting her and then sat back and studied her face carefully. "Are you sure that you're all right Molly? If you aren't feeling well, we can go home."

"I just need some food. I'll be quite all right when I've eaten I'm sure."

The wine arrived and she wondered at the advisability of drinking it on an empty stomach. But it was chilled and felt cool and soothing as she sipped it. Within a few minutes she felt much better, less tired, quite chatty, if somewhat lightheaded. She began to relax and even smiled at JC. His answering smile was heartwarming and she felt carefree for the first time in ages.

"We haven't done very well in finding what we wanted, have we?"

"There is still the afternoon and tomorrow, if need be. We'll find what we want somewhere."

"But there are no more stores that sell furniture."

"Oh, yes, there are lots of them. We aren't confined to shopping right here in town you know."

"Where are we going then?"

He named a couple of cities that were within an hour's drive and even mentioned some that were further away.

"That will take most of the afternoon and tomorrow, to, I would think. Aren't they closed on Sunday?"

"Several of the larger stores have afternoon shopping on Sunday. I would hope that we can finish today, but if we don't then we'll do it tomorrow."

Molly suddenly remembered Tim Murphy. It didn't look like she'd be going to the beach with him after all. Had JC heard enough of her conversation with Tim to figure out their plans she wondered?

"I was to have tomorrow off."

"Yes, you were, aren't you? I suppose that I could choose the furniture myself, I'd really rather have you along for the woman's point of view. Well, we shall have to hope that we can find what we need today. If not, then we'll discuss an alternative tomorrow."

The wine was making Molly really mellowed by now and instead of bristling, as you might have ordinarily done, she smiled at him again with warmth and said, "it really doesn't matter. I haven't made any definite plans for tomorrow. I'm sure this is more important." Her hands rested on the table and he covered them with one of his. Somehow the touch felt as intimate to her as his lips had felt on hers the night before.

"I appreciate that, Molly. Let's hope that we don't have to use up your whole day."

"Now that I have some more wine, please."

He his head. "Despite how much I'm enjoying the mood it has induced him you, I think you'd better eat first. Maybe later on."

She blushed. "Is it that obvious?"

"I think it's the first time that you have ever appeared at ease in my presence, Molly. I would like to see more of it, hopefully not only with the help of alcohol."

They ordered lunch and a leisurely, a pleasant glow still lingering from the wine she had drunk. When they had finished, he took her arm and guided her back to the car. She resisted the urge to press even closer to him than that.

It was a struggle to keep her eyes open and her mind from

drifting as they drove along in the smooth riding car. He had opened the roof and the air was fresh and warm on her head resting back against the soft leather of the seat. He looked at her and smiled lazily. "Poor Molly, if we didn't have to get that room ready in such a short time, I would take you home now and let you have that nap you're dying for, but not until I took advantage of the effect that wine seemed to have on you."

"What do you mean?"

Don't ask foolish questions, darling."

Molly felt that she should protest his remark, but the effort was too much and she just closed her eyes and let the warmth of the sun and the warmth that was stealing over her body have their way. She knew what he meant, and she knew that a word or a touch would make him change his mind. She was more than a little tempted to make that move, but somehow just knowing that she had that power was enough for now and she let her mind slip into oblivion.

She fought being roused from the dream in which her tall, fair tormentor had become loving in the warmth of his arms was more desirable than anything she had ever experienced. Her conscious mind took over, but the warmth remained. This warmth was too solid, too real to be a dream.

"Molly," whispered the voice against her ear and his warm breath caressed her sensitive skin. She was resting against him where she must have leaned, or been pulled, while she was sleeping. "Molly, we're here. Wake up now."

She opened her eyes slowly to meet his. The message in them brought a flash of heat from her toes to her brow. She struggled to sit up bright and get away from the effect he had on her at this close range. He smiled ruefully. "I knew I should have taken you home."

"Where are we?" She tried to change the subject, distract him from observing her agitation.

"We're in Keene, dammit. Get out and we'll see what they have to offer." His mood was as mercurial as her own, she thought.

They managed to find glass topped tables and wrought iron chairs in white that were similar to the ones by the pool, but smaller, or the balcony. JC ordered another set for the balcony outside the other guest rooms, to be delivered at a later date. After two more stops, they had acquired a chrome and glass writing table and a phone in the same shade of gray as the room. It was nearing 5 o'clock and closing time for most of the establishments on a Saturday, so he decided that they should head for home and leave the television cabinet for the next day. He agreed and they drove home in the near silence, though it was about a 45 minute drive. She thought about their earlier, lighter mood and wished that it were back.

When they pulled into the garage, he broke the long silence.

"Since I have used up your whole day, and it has been a long one, I feel I should take you out to eat rather than making you prepare a meal."

She was reluctant to spend more time with him when they were both so tense with each other. "That's not necessary. I have some frozen dishes prepared ahead. It won't take long to heat were in the microwave."

"No, I insist. Click on that dress and will go to a nice place I know. Will a half hour be long enough? I'll change and make sure we have reservations."

She knew the futility of arguing further, so she nodded and got out of the car, going directly to her room to shower and change. This was going to be an evening that she would always remember, she felt, for better or for worse.

8 CHAPTER EIGHT

The restaurant he had chosen was in a small resort town about a 20 minute drive away. Although Molly had traveled over this same road numerous times in her life, the sign indicating that it was the John Stark highway had never really captured her attention before. Being used she turned to JC's attention was on the road ahead and said, "how does it feel to have a road with the same name as you have?"

He gave her a quick glance and grin. "When I first came here, I noticed that right away and did some research. It would seem that Gen. John Stark wasn't New Hampshire hero of sorts. Of course not of the same stature as Daniel Webster, but he did make a name for himself during the Revolutionary war."

Molly nodded, "we had to learn about him in school as part of our state's history. I don't remember much about him except that at one point he became a very put out that he was not promoted as quickly as he thought he should be and got angry and returned to his home. His wife's name was Molly Stark. I remember that because everyone in class looked at me and laughed when we read about it."

JC glanced her way again. "It would be amusing to youngsters I presume. Life seems to be full of coincidences doesn't it, Molly?"

"Yes, lately it does."

They arrived at the small hotel nestled among the birches of the lake. A week or so them to a table overlooking the water. The dining room was about half full of minors and Molly noticed at one end of the dining room the wall and floor.

She wondered, as they were seated, what the other people in the thought as a as we and followed the tall man in the girl with pink dress with their eyes. Would they be surprised to find out that it was an employer and its housekeeper and not a married couple or lovers out for an evening of dining and dancing?

JC ordered wine for Molly and a cocktail for himself. She said at the cool liquid and hope that it would relax her a bit, but the alcohol did not take affect the way it had that afternoon.

The meal was superbly cooked and was and she made a mental note of the ingredients that were used in some of the dishes for future reference in her own cooking. More wine accompanied the meal and JC ordered a liqueur to go with the dessert.

Their conversation was pleasant, but decidedly stilted and Molly found herself keeping her eyes directed to the setting sun and then the rising moon as they were reflected on the mirror smooth surface of the lake, rather than on JC's face. It was easier on her nerves and served to restore some serenity to her tempestuous emotions. She knew that if her eyes met his directly, he would read some of the tumult that was there.

The band members entered and began tuning their instruments. Molly noticed that some of the ill maintained sipping cocktails, while others had been replaced by a 20s and 30s age group who were there for drinks and dancing now that the dinner hour was over.

"Would you care to stay and a dance?"

Molly was prepared for the question. "I'll leave it to you, JC. You've had a long day, too."

"We'll stay a while then." He signaled the cocktail waitress and ordered scotch for himself and asked Molly what she would have. She still didn't feel any effects from the wine they had had with dinner, but decided that it might not be wise change to a different beverage, so she ordered white wine. By the time their drinks arrived, the band was in full swing and several couples were occupying the small dance floor. They sipped their drinks and watched.

The next number was slow and he stood and helped Molly to her feet. They walked the few steps to the dance floor. Molly turned to face him and raised her arms. His eyes held hers for a fraction of a second, then pulled her close and their bodies moved together to the rhythm of the music. He was holding her so closely, that holding her head back was too much of an effort and she let it rest lightly against him. The little floor was crowded, but they might have been alone for all the attention she gave to the others around them. It was like drifting on gentle waves and she wished that the music would never and. But of course it did. He kept his arm about her waist as he guided her back to their table.

She missed her wine and ordered that both breath. He thought that maybe he would regret it the next morning, but did not. She resolved to sip it very slowly.

"John, what are you doing here?"

Molly's back was to the speaker, but she knew Tim Murphy's voice. She blushed in anticipation of his reaction when he realized who his boss's companion was.

"Hello, Tim," JC's voice was as calm as could be. "Molly has been working above and beyond the call of duty, though I am treating her to dinner. The poor girl has to work tomorrow also, I'm afraid."

Molly felt the telltale flush coming over her, and reluctantly looked up to face Tim's surprised eyes. He quickly recovered and introduced JC and Molly is the pert redhead that accompanied him. She was about Molly's age and looked like a typical coed in her casual, but flattering outfit which accented her well endowed bosom. JC, who had stood when Tim addressed him, gestured to the two empty chairs at their table. "Will you join us, or would you prefer a more private table? We will not be staying much longer anyway, as we have a busy day ahead of us tomorrow."

"Thanks, we don't you, Tim replied, "we just came to dance and the place seems pretty full." Molly avoided Tim's eyes and she quickly finished the glass of wine that she had meant make glass. More drinks were ordered and she and JC and again, being joined on the floor by Kim and the girl he had introduced as BJ. They are as they can, but somehow the magic of had disappeared.

Him as Molly more than and she could think of no great reviews, though she noticed the look of impatient across JC's face. He asked BJ to dance and both couples went to the dance floor.

"You evidently don't have tomorrow free after all," Tim said. He held her as closely as JC had, but she made the effort to keep her head back a bit from his shoulder.

"No, JC's grandmother is coming to stay for a while and we

are getting her room ready. We couldn't find everything we needed today and she is arriving Monday. I guess I'll have to take a rain check on the beach, Tim."

"I think if he has anything to say about it, it will keep right on raining," he muttered.

"What do you mean?"

"John is a good boss. I enjoy working for him. But I think he is trying to tell me something and I don't like it."

"I don't know what you mean, Tim."

"I've got a feeling you'll know soon enough, if you don't have some idea already. Are you his private territory, Molly?"

"Of course not! What a thing to say! He's my boss and that is all there is to it. I've only known him for a week!"

"A week can be a long time, you know. Why I can accomplish quite a lot in a week. Forget I said that, will you?"

"I wish you hadn't said any of it, Tim. I don't think I like your inferences about JC and me at all. In fact, that's why his grandmother is coming to stay, at least in part. JC was afraid that people would talk because I'm young and all. I certainly didn't expect it of you, though."

Molly was feeling the wine quite strongly now, and she looked Tim squarely in the eye. He flushed this time. "I'm sorry, Molly. I didn't mean to make you feel uncomfortable or to infer that there was anything going on. Please forgive me. Chalk it up to jealousy."

"BJ seems like a nice girl. Have you known her long?"

He grinned, his natural good humor restored. "Since I met her at the beach this afternoon."

Molly grinned back. "Then I guess you won't have to spend the day in solitude tomorrow after all, will you."

"Touché."

The music ended and they returned to their table. They sipped their drinks and sat out a couple of fast numbers, neither Tim nor JC seeming interested in that kind of music. Then another slow tune began and JC said, "come on, Molly, one last dance and then we better head home."

When she stood this time, she realized that all the wine she had drunk had caught up with her at once and she swayed against JC as she stood up. He caught her close to his side and his hold was firm as he guided her to the floor. As they began to dance, she raised her face to his and smiled ruefully, all her inhibitions gone,

"I feel like Cinderella tonight. I must be home by midnight and then Prince charming will disappear."

"I think not. That is if you choose for him not to."

His cheek rested against hers and she couldn't feel the floor anymore. "JC," she murmured.

"Yes, Molly?"

"I really have had too much to drink. I feel like we're dancing on air."

"Then perhaps I've had too much to drink, too."

"Tim asked me if I was your territory."

"And you said?"

"I told him the truth."

"And what is the truth, Molly?"

"I told him that was silly. I'm your housekeeper and I've only known you a week."

"And he said?"

"He apologized for his remarks. He really is quite a decent fellow, you know. I hope you won't hold it against him. That he said what he did, I mean."

"Don't worry about it, Molly. Just relax and enjoy the dance and stopped chattering."

"I'm sorry. My tongue always gets loose when I drink, which isn't often."

He kept his cheek against hers until they finished the dance, and when it was over, he didn't see her again, but bade a quick farewell to Tim and BJ and escorted her out.

The moon was so bright that it was almost like daylight when they emerged from the hotel. She drank in the cool, fresh air and tried to make her had come back onto her shoulders. JC took her arm and led her to the car.

"Thank you for dinner and the lovely evening. I haven't danced since college, I don't think. It was enjoyable."

"I'm glad you liked it Molly. I enjoyed this evening also."

Sleepiness had left Molly, and she felt almost hyperactive, not wanting to let go of the night that she felt would not ever come again.

When they pulled up in front gleaming white light, Molly was eyes when JC stopped the car outside of putting it in the garage she looked at him quizzically. "Are you going somewhere?"

"I guess that depends on you, Cinderella. It's only 11. That leaves you an hour before the coach turns into a pumpkin. Would you care for a stroll in the moonlight before the bewitching hour?"

She nodded. "I'd like that," she said softly.

They got out and he took her hand. They started walking across the lawn, slightly damp with dew. "Are you cold, Molly?" He asked.

"No, I'm quite comfortable. The coolness feels good with all the alcohol I've had."

They wandered across the lawn to the edge of the trees and Molly found herself telling him about her refuge when things were difficult at home and how she had stumbled on one here. He asked to be led there, and beneath the bright white light of the moon she managed to find a spot quite easily. Only traces of the silvery beams penetrated the canopy of leaves and it took a minute for her eyes to adjust to the dark shadows around them.

"Isn't this a gorgeous place?" She breathed. "I can't wait for fall when the leaves turn."

His hand still held hers and it tightened and brought hers to his lips. "Your Prince charming is honored at being allowed to share your private paradise, Cinderella."

"You're quite welcome, your Majesty. She made a deep curtsy, and as she rose, she was drawn close against him, his lips seeking hers. Her arms went around his neck and she lost herself in the ecstasy of the embrace. She clung to him, letting him mold her live body to his with complete abandon. She parted her lips and let him invade the mouse that hungered for him. She stroked the back of his neck and moaned softly in her throat as an aching desire grew in her, intensifying until she struggled to suppress the sob that rose in her throat.

His mouth left hers and moved to her ear. His breath was warm as he murmured against the delicate low, "here, Molly, or back at the house?"

She didn't have to ask what he meant. She knew. She couldn't answer with words. She could hardly breathe, so intense was the desire that swept her body, and when his hand found its way inside the bodice of her dress and touched the tender flashing of her breast, a tremor wracked her body. She helped him finish unbuttoning the material that obstructed his flesh from hers and when the pink silk dress rested in a pool about her feet he discarded the scrap of lace that covered the thrusting, throbbing breasts. A silver shaft of light through the leaves eliminated the aroused, rosy nipples and he gasped as he stared at the beauty before him. Then his caressing mouth descended, and developing one of the delicate morsels and she felt she would swoon with the rapture that overtook her.

"Oh, JC, please help me, please," she pleaded. His mouse sought the other breast and she's pulled at his close in urgency.

A sudden sharp blast pierced the night, Molly protested when his head rose reluctantly from caressing her body. The blast was repeated again and again and her stunned mind was brought back to earth with a crash. Someone was blowing a car horn insistently and the sound was coming from the direction of the house. JC swore softly and looked down at her half naked figure with agony in his eyes.

"What is it?" She whispered, a shiver going through her body which had been consumed by fire only moments before.

"I don't know, but it damn well better be important," she said through clenched teeth. He pulled off his blazer and wrapped it around her shoulders. "Stay here, darling, and I'll see what's up. I'll either call you or come back, and believe me, I hope it's the latter."

He turned and ran quickly through the trees toward the house. The blaring horn ceased and she waited for what seemed like a lifetime, straining her ears for any sound or voice. She was about to dress and see for herself what was going on, when she heard the rustling of leaves and he entered the bower they had shared so intimately a short while earlier.

"What was it?" She asked, pulling his jacket closer about her.

He pulled her close against him and kissed her firmly and then put her from him. "It was your sister. Your father has had a crisis and she feels your mother needs you. Come up to the house and put on something warmer and I'll take you to your mother."

"Is Maria still here? What's wrong?"

"I sent Maria back. We are alone so you don't have to worry about your state of undress. She tried calling and when she couldn't get anyone, she came up. The car was here and she couldn't rouse anyone with the doorbell, so she decided to use the car horn." He bent and picked up her discarded clothing and, taking her hand, they went back to the house. He said he had a call to make and that she should dress quickly and be ready to go in a few minutes.

She replaced her bra and pulled on a pair of slacks and a

cotton sweater. She repaired her lipstick and ran a comb through her disheveled hair. She wondered, as she looked at her flushed face in the mirror, if this crisis had saved her from one of her own or torn her from of bewitched world that she might never enter again.

"Molly, are you ready?" JC appeared at her doorway.

"Yes, I'm ready. She paced him in the brilliance of the light from the overhead lamp and he said softly, "I am sorry, Molly. So very sorry." He didn't say why he was sorry and there was no time to ask. When they were in the car and headed down the hill, he said grimly, "you're going to have to be ready to face a very difficult situation, Molly."

"Did my father leave again?"

"Worse, I'm afraid. He was released from the hospital this morning and he tried to take his own life."

Molly gasped, "what happened? Is he-"

he took one hand off the wheel and squeezed hers that were clasped in her lap. "The gunshot was not fatal, but he is in serious condition. Your mother is at the hospital and I am taking you there. Your brother and sister are with her, but I am sure they will all take comfort from your being with them."

"My mother must be frantic. When did it happen?"

I talked to the hospital on the phone and they told me that he was brought in about 9 o'clock tonight. He has lost a lot of blood, but as far as they can determine, has an excellent chance of recovering if he will cooperate and have the will to live. He is sedated and has had several transfusions."

"What a terrible experience for mother and the kids to go through! I can't help but think that if I had been there, maybe it wouldn't have happened." Silent tears stole down her cheeks.

"There is nothing that you could have done, except lend them moral support. There is no need for you to have any guilty feelings at all. Your father is obviously very ill and the only thing you can do is comfort your family and pray that he will recover, not only from this incident, but with psychiatric treatment and counseling."

They pulled into the almost deserted parking lot of the hospital, and Molly scrambled out of the car almost before he could shut off the engine. He caught up with her on the steps outside the door. "Molly, before you go in, remember what I said and that I will be right there if you need me."

She nodded and wiped her eyes. They entered the hushed waiting room and JC inquired at the desk where they should go. The nurse on duty gave him some instructions in a low voice which Molly didn't hear. He nodded and, taking her arm, led her down the long, dim the corridor to the left. At the end of the hall was another nurses station and JC told the nurse who Molly was. She told them to go through a set of swinging doors on the right and they would find her family in a waiting room there.

Molly's mother was slumped in a chair, looking like she had faced about all that one person could shoulder in a lifetime. Mike was pacing back and forth and Maria, her eyes swollen from crying, looked up from a magazine she was thumbing through.

"Molly! I'm so glad you're here!" She exclaimed and jumping up, threw herself into her sister's arms. Molly held her sister and her eyes met her mother's tortured ones.

"Molly, I just don't know why he did such a thing," she said. She had obviously used up all her tears in the several hours since the terrible event and seemed entirely spent of all emotion.

Molly gently pushed Maria aside and sat down beside her mother. "He'll be all right, mom, I'm sure. JC talked with the doctor in charge and he said is chances are good."

Her mother nodded, "that's what he told me, but there has just been so much lately, that I can't be very optimistic, I'm afraid."

JC spoke and his calm, firm voice demanded all their attention. "There is really nothing that we can gain by staying here. If there is any change in Mr. Stark's condition, I'm sure they will notify us immediately. Why don't I take all of you home, either to your house or mine, and we will have some coffee and some rest so you can be ready to face tomorrow."

Mrs. Stark shook her head. "I just can't leave right now."

Molly's eyes met JC's "I will stay with mother." Her eyes pleaded with his to understand what she must do. He nodded silently and turned to the others.

"Come on kids, I'll take you home. I'm sure that there are things we can do their to make your mother and father's homecoming more comfortable."

Mike and Maria had been at the hospital for several hours now and their eyes showed relief at the suggestion. Molly added, "yes, go with JC. I'll stay with mom and we'll call you if there is any change in dad's condition, or if we need anything."

JC, might you. Molly tried unsuccessfully mother son. He didn't sleep, it's that sort of her and Molly became concerned as the night on the right hand of the at two, and the and Molly stood anxiously to hear any report that he might give.

"Mrs. Stark?"

Molly gestured to her mother who still sat in the chair staring straight ahead. The doctor went over to her mother and put his hand on her shoulder he shook her gently, "Mrs. Stark, your husband is doing nicely now. The wound is a flesh wound and no vital organs are affected. He is sleeping and will for some hours. You really should go home now and get some rest so you will be strong and ready to encourage him when he awakes."

Mrs. Stark shook her head, as though trying to bring herself back to reality. She looked at the doctor and spoke for the first time in hours. "Are you sure?"

"Yes, Mrs. Stark, I'm as sure as any of us can be in a case like this."

Molly went over to her mother. "Let me take you home, mom. JC took the kids home and I know they are anxious to hear some news and have you there. They need you to help them through this you know."

"Of course, they do. I got so wrapped up in my own troubles, I'm afraid I forgot that they would be equally upset."

A nurse stepped into the room and asked, "which one of you is Molly Stark? There is a phone call for you."

Molly identified herself and followed the nurse out to the desk.

"Hello."

JC's voice answered her. "How is everything, Molly?"

"The doctor just came in and said that dad is going to be all right. He is trying to get mom to go home and get some rest.

"That sounds like a good idea and for you, too."

"I'm pretty sure that she will agree. I mentioned that the kids needed her right now."

"Are you all right to drive, or shall I come for you? I brought the kids home in your parents' car and left mind for you. The keys are with the nurse at the desk in the waiting room."

Molly almost smiled at the thought of JC driving the awkward sedan when he was used to such high performance machines.

"I'm fine to drive. I should be right along."

"I have put the kids to work and even managed to do some cleaning up myself, so everything is quite presentable here. I'll put on some fresh coffee and expect you soon."

"Hopefully, in just a few minutes. My mom drinks tea, so heat some water for that if you would."

"You got it."

Molly's mother was persuaded to leave and she breathed a deep sigh, almost of relief, when they stepped out into the chilly air of the early morning hours. She was impressed with the car, which Molly had never driven before, but which was so effortless in the deserted streets, that she didn't feel nervous about driving it, though it was far bigger than she was used to handling.

The lights were a blaze in the little house, with the porch lights on in welcome. JC, Mike and Maria all sat at the kitchen table and gave them a warm welcome when they entered. Coffee and tea were waiting in the atmosphere became almost relaxed as they sat in the little kitchen and shared the hot beverages and the support of each other.

When Mike and Maria seemed to be nodding, from exhaustion, JC sent them to bed and suggested that Mrs. Stark and Molly had better get some rest also. Molly nodded and walked to the door with him. They stepped out on the porch and she said quietly, "I hope you don't mind my staying here for what's left of the night. I really don't want to leave mom right now."

"I mind like hell, Molly, but I know you feel you have to do it. Get some sleep and don't worry about anything. I'll be by in the morning and hopefully everything will be better." He raised her chin and kissed her lightly. "Oh, Molly, what might have been," he said so softly that she almost didn't hear it.

She felt herself blush and quickly said, "good night, JC" she watched him climb into the car and waved as he drove off.

Molly got her mother into bed and curled up on the couch under an afghan with the telephone on the table beside her. She didn't think sleep would ever come, but it did, deep and dreamless.

Insistent wrapping on the kitchen door brought her out of her dreamless sleep and it took her a minute to get her bearings. Then she remembered where she was, and white, and she hastily threw aside the afghan and hurried to the door. A deep sense of relief flooded her tense body when she saw JC on the other side of the screen door.

He grinned at her and she looked down ruefully at the wrinkled slacks and tried to smooth her rumpled hair. "Since you were home to cook for me, I decided to come here for breakfast."

She unhooked the door and opened it. He came in carrying her shabby suitcase in one hand and a bag bearing a fast food logo in the other.

"I figured you'd welcome a change of clothes, so I brought some things of yours. I hope I managed to include everything you need."

"Thank you. I really do need to take a shower and change."

"I called the hospital and your father is still considered out of immediate danger. He is asleep and there is nothing anyone can do further at the moment. You get dressed. I'll make coffee and then we can indulge in some of these goodies."

Molly tiptoed up the stairs, hoping not to wake any of her exhausted family, but her mother called as she passed the bedroom door and she stopped to reassure her that everything was fine. She showered and put on the close that JC had brought. She flushed when she thought of him going through her drawers to come up with the lacy bra and briefs. Then last night in the grove flashback through her mind and her color deepened.

When she went back down to the kitchen, she felt almost shy about facing him, so vivid was her memory of what had happened and what had almost happened. It had seemed so natural, so right in that setting, but now in the light of day she began to wonder what he thought of her.

"Feel better?"

She nodded and reached for the coffee that he held out to her. He gestured to the place he had set for her at the table and she sat down. A Styrofoam container with scrambled eggs, bacon and an English muffin sat before her and at first she thought she would be able to eat, but he sat down and started eating with gusto and she found that she was hungry after all. "I'm sorry about all this disruption in your plans, and with your grandmother coming at all."

"There is no need for you to concern yourself over it, Molly. You had no control over it happening and getting ready for grandmother's visit must seem very insignificant in comparison. I see no reason why you can't return home later today, if all goes well. Your family will have to learn to get along without you here sooner or later, you know."

She nodded. "I know that, but this has been such a shock for everyone."

"Sometimes that's what it takes to get some people's life together, unfortunately. Your mother is going to have to make some hard decisions, but they must be hers alone and not what you or the other kids think."

"You're right, of course, but it somehow seems very cruel to make her face it right now."

"If she had faced it sooner, this might not have happened."

Molly felt herself blush again. "Do you mean that I didn't do her any favors by staying and helping out."

"No, Molly, I'm sure you felt you had to and I don't think it had any effect on what happened with your father. But she's going to have to let you go sooner or later and if you don't make that clear to her, the road for your brother and sister is not going to be any easier than yours has been."

The rest of the family came down and joined them. Mike and Maria were enthusiastic about the breakfast waiting for them, but Mrs. Stark ate little. JC took Molly and her mother to the hospital and they left her mother there to await her father's waking up. They returned to his house and he suggested that Molly prepare a dinner for her family and he would bring them all back to eat that afternoon.

"JC, what about the rest of the shopping for your grandmother's room?"

"If I can't take care of it before I leave tomorrow, then I'll leave it up to you to come up with something. If you are busy doing that, you won't have so much energy to waste worrying."

Molly busied herself preparing a meal and setting the dining room table which JC insisted that they should use for so much company. Molly thought how impressed her family would be with the elegant surroundings, especially Maria. Mike would think it was all very nice, but the contents of the garage would be of more interest to him than the furnishings in the house.

At noon JC went to the hospital to get Mrs. Stark and she called Mike and Maria and told them to come and to bring their bathing suits as there should be time to swim before dinner.

The car was in the yard in a matter of minutes with both teenagers gazing in our at the new residents where their sister now lived they were marveling over the hall and kitchen, when JC and their mother arrives. JC said that he would join the kids in a swim, while Molly finished the dinner preparations and talked with her mother.

Mr. Stark had woken up for a few minutes and he had known her and try to say a few words. She felt greatly relieved at the amount of progress. Molly let her help with getting the dinner ready, as she knew that she needed something to occupy the usually busy hands that had been so futilely idle for the past few hours.

At two they all sat down at the table, resplendent in crystal, silver and fine China, and even Mrs. Stark ate a creditable amount of food, under the circumstances.

JC took Mike out to the garage to check out the cars and tractor more closely and the three women made quick work of restoring the dining room and kitchen to order. Molly took Maria and her mother on a tour of the house, which impressed them greatly. Mrs. Stark side as she said, "I can understand why you want to keep this job, Molly. The house is so beautiful and Mr. Stark is so nice. I just hope that you don't let it all go to your head and forget that it's just a job."

The comment surprised Molly. She hadn't thought of her mother worrying about how she might get involved and get her. Could she read her mind, she wondered or was it just a lucky guess?

"Don't worry about me, mom. My feet are on the ground. This is a job and I like it and it pays well. JC has been very kind and I really appreciate his concern for you and the kids. I won't let the stars get in my eyes to the point that I can't handle it."

Maria looked from one to the other with questioning eyes. Their conversation was going over her head and yet she sensed that what they were not saying was more important than the words they spoke. "Are you in love with Mr. Stark, Molly?" She gasped.

Out of the mouths of babes, thought Molly and she turned to leave them down the stairs, hoping they hadn't seen the flush that swept her face. "He's my boss, Maria, and a very attractive man, but not in my league at all." She was going to add some more, but stopped with a quick intake of breath as JC loomed before her around the bend in the staircase. She could feel her color deep and even more at his surprise appearance and she wondered how much, if any he had heard.

In any case, she knew that he missed nothing of her telltale face and she blurted, "I've just shown mother and Maria the upstairs."

He stood there, blocking the stairs and making her feel about as uncomfortable as she had ever felt in her life. His eyes refused to release hers or let her burning face returned to normal. It seemed like forever before he broke the spell. "I thought your mother might like to return to the hospital now and that you might come along to, Molly."

"Oh, yes, I really should get back, Molly," her mother said from this their above her.

JC turned and they all descended the rest of the staircase. Mike and Maria had decided to follow in the family car in case they were allowed to visit their father.

Molly sat in the back seat and listen to JC and her mother carry on a conversation. She could think of nothing to add, in fact her thoughts were not on what they were saying at all. JC help them both out of the car in her mother hurried in ahead of them, anxious for any new developments that might have taken place while she was away. JC took Molly's arm and held her to his own very slow pace as they walked to the hospital door.

"I don't think it would be wise for you to go in and see your father, even if he's awake, Molly."

She nodded. If he were still upset with her, it could only cause a possible setback and she didn't want to feel responsible for that.

"We'll go in and check on his condition and then I think you'd better come home and get some rest. You didn't have much last night and now we have grandmother coming.

"I am feeling a little tired, but I'll be all right."

"Yes, you'll be all right. I know how well you hold up with a lot on your shoulders, but I don't like the circles under your eyes and see no need for you to go without another night of rest in your own bed instead of on a lumpy sofa."

"I can sleep anywhere when I'm really tired. The sofa didn't bother me at all."

"Well I want you rested when you meet grandmother. She misses nothing at all and if she were to see you now, she would accuse me of being an insensitive slave driver."

Molly's father was awake and her mother had gone into be with him, so Molly and JC left, having told the nurses to have her mother call and keep them posted on his condition.

Back at the house, JC told Molly to go to her room and get some sleep. He had calls to make and would fix himself a snack if she slept through the supper hour. She went willingly, exhaustion stealing over her so that she just fell on the bed and was almost instantly asleep. She heard JC come in for a minute to check on her, but her mind wouldn't let her mouth respond. She didn't catch all of his quiet comment, but was quite sure he had ended it with "Little Leaguer." She'd have to think about what that meant when she woke up.

9 CHAPTER NINE

When she will it was dark and she could hear no sounds in the house. She reached for the lamp beside the bed, and when her eyes became accustomed to the light, saw that it was eleven-thirty. She had slept for six hours! She went into the bathroom and splashed some cool water on her face. She decided that she needed something to eat. There was no sign of light in the hall, living room or kitchen and she thought that JC must have gone to bed. She knew he planned on going to Boston the next day and he had not had a great deal of sleep the night before either.

She patted silently in her bare feet across the cool marble floor and turned on the main kitchen light. The coffee maker had some left in it, and JC had left it turned on, which meant it was still hot. She poured herself a cup and then went to the refrigerator to see what she could find that look tempting. She took out the roast beef that was left from dinner and made a fixed sandwich which he carried, with her coffee, to the table.

She didn't hear him enter, but sensed his eyes on her. She looked up, her mouth full of her first bite of the sandwich.

"That looks mighty good. Do we have more?"

She nodded and finished chewing and swallowing. "You didn't eat any supper did you?"

He grinned. "No, I kept thinking you wake up and we had such a big dinner that I wasn't in danger of perishing."

Molly got up and made another sandwich while he poured coffee and sat down in his usual spot across from her place.

"Did my mother call when I was asleep?"

"She called to say that your father is doing nicely and that they are hopeful of a complete recovery in a short while."

"I'm glad. She really needs some good news for a change."

"Let's hope that it's all good news from now on. While he's in the hospital, your mother and the doctor are arranging for some AA hopefully he can be influenced to admit his problem, face it and lick it."

"I hope so. It would be such a relief for the whole family and he must hate being this way himself."

"It's all up to him now. There is nothing that anyone else can do if she doesn't have the motivation."

Molly put the sandwich in front of him and he ate hungrily. She finished her own food and asked if he would like anything else.

"Do we have any I left from the other night?"

"We do and less you've eaten it."

"Then I think I'll have a piece of that."

She got out the pie and cut them each a generous wedge and refilled their cups and sat down again.

"You should get to bed if you are leaving for Boston bright and early." He looked up from the high he had been concentrating on "grandmother's flight is due at six. I plan to leave noon and put in a few hours at the office before picking her up. Then, as I said I think it will need best if we stay over come up here today, probably in the afternoon."

"There is still the cabinet for her television and that's supposed to be delivered tomorrow."

"I know. When they arrived, they can just connect it and leave it on the floor. When we find the proper piece of furniture to hold it, I'm sure we can manage to put it in."

She nodded thoughtfully. "I still have to get the magazines you wanted for her and I thought that the writing table should be stocked with stationery and stamps and the like."

"You're right. That would be a good idea. You can take care of that tomorrow afternoon and Tuesday you can put some fresh flowers in her room. She's particularly fond of daisies and violets because they remind her of her childhood when she found them wild and picked them for her own mother."

"There should be plenty around here to be picked. I'm sure I can handle that. Is she your mother's mother or your father's mother?"

"My father's. Another Stark in the household, I'm afraid. I'm particularly close to her because when my parents were killed, she and my grandfather took me to their home."

"I'm sorry. I didn't realize that your parents weren't living."

"There was no way for you to know, since I never mentioned it. I was about the same age as your brother when they were in an automobile accident. Mom was killed immediately and dad lived for a week. My brother and I were split up because my other grandparents insisted on having one of us."

"That sounds almost cruel. Were you able to see much of each other."

"He was two years younger than I am and as the two sets of grandparents lived in Massachusetts and New York, we didn't get together very often. We kept in touch by phone and writing and when I went off to college, I chose one close to where he was. These were four good years, as I could go help him with his homework and watch them play sports and he could attend the games I played in. Naturally, he enrolled in the same college."

"Where is he now?"

A dark look crossed his face, and Molly wished that she hadn't asked. "He loved sports. Anything athletic had to be tried. A little over a year ago he was killed while mountain climbing in Colorado."

"I'm sorry. That must have seemed like a very bitter blow when he was all you had left." She thought about the pictures in the album and realize now that the other handsome man in the photos must of been his brother.

"Yes, it was. When Jeff died, I felt a need to get away for a while and I bought this house and used it for a retreat. The fact that our business, which became mine when he died, had an office here made it ideal. I could be by myself and still keep in touch with the operations." You both must have very good business had to be so successful so young."

"We worked well together, which they say is unusual for most brother. I think one of the reasons was that we only had each other and had spent those six years apart. My parents left us enough money to get started, and some investment that we made paid off handsomely. I still keep the original company that we started together, but spend most of my and other people's investments now."

"Is that why you had no help here except the Friday lady and the gardener? I mean, because you wanted to be alone."

"Yes, to start with. And then after a few months I began to spend more time in the city and less here. This summer I decided that the country life and air is more to my liking, but I couldn't just live here alone and keep everything the way it should be and entertain and the like. I had just spent a couple of weeks in the Bahamas and when I got back I didn't have time to spend searching for help. I decided that no one in the city would want to come up here, and if they did they might have difficulty adjusting, so I took a chance on asking neighbors about help and that is how I came to call you."

They had finished their pie and he asked if she still was interested in the photo albums. She got up eagerly, "let me just take care of these dishes and I'd love to." They went to the den and through into his private room. For almost an hour he showed her photos of his family and friends and when they came to the ones of Joan she wanted to ask more but didn't dare. She was almost afraid of what he might say.

When they had closed the last of the books, he went to the bar and poured himself a drink "would you like something, Molly? A little wine, perhaps?"

"No, thank you. I think after yesterday I'd better not."

He thought for a minute and then grinned. He held his glass up in the saloon and said, "here's to you, Cinderella," and he took a long drink.

Molly turned and headed for the door, knowing he had seen the beginning of the rosy hue that flooded her face. "Thank you for showing me the pictures. I think I'd better go to bed now and so had you."

"If I thought that was meant as an invitation, I jumped at the chance. But since I know you better than that, I think I'll sit here with my memories for a while first. Sleep tight, Little Leaguer."

Molly almost ran through the dark den and living room. So it hadn't been her imagination and he had heard what she had said to her mother, part of it anyway. She slammed her bedroom door and cursed as she stubbed her bare toe on the bedside table. She had slept long enough to make her wide-awake and she felt the need to work off her frustration and confusion. She pulled off her clothes and left them in a heap on the floor which was quite an customary of her. She donned the bikini and slipped quietly out the door to the pool. JC always kept the drapes pulled at night in his "inner sanctum" and she knew he planned on staying there for a while.

She eased herself into the water so there would be no splash for him to hear, but her mind was more at ease. Grandmother was coming and she only had to get through a few more hours before there would be a third person around the house to ease the tension and put things aback in perspective. When she a while, she sank back in the comfort of the water, which was more than the air. This time she swam slowly, taking time to float and looked up are. She reached for the ladder to pull herself out and a warm dry hand closed over her wet one. She gasped in surprise.

"I went to your room to speak to you and you weren't there. When I saw your door open, I figured you must be out here."

"I wasn't sleepy and thought a swim would work off some of my frustrations." The words slipped out without her thinking about how it might sound to him.

"Are you frustrated, Molly? Why?"

He helped her out of the water and she wished now that she had stayed in it.

"Oh, everything that's happened the past week is catching up with me, I guess. I'm fine now. What did you want to speak to me about."

She wanted to move further away from him, but his hand held her arm firmly.

"I wanted to tell you that I didn't mean to upset you as I seem to have done. Sometimes I forget that you're really still just a kid and that some of the things I say to you only should be said to a woman, or not at all."

"I am not a kid, JC, I'm not!" The fury that filled her surprised even Molly herself. "I'm not a kid and apparently you didn't think so last night." She yanked the string at the back of her neck that held the brought to her bikini up, and the wet garment fell exposing the proud breasts, the chill making the nipples stand erect. The fact that he said nothing, did not move, made her anger flared even higher. "Do you think you were the first man to ever touch or look at me? I was a college girl, remember, and that was two years ago. Tim Murphy doesn't think of me as a child. If I had gone with him today, I'll bet-"

cursed roughly the number so well. She pushed against, and personal, so that the was in the around the flat as I usually felt when he touched her. He can only succeed of him as they met with the on muscle.

His hand held holders in the grass and he held her at arms length "I am going to make allowances for tonight because you have had a difficult day, but if you ever talk to me like that again, you will pay dearly for it."

His hard voice brought some sanity back to her, enough so that she tried ineffectively to call the bit of material up over her breasts again. But his arms were still cruelly tight on her shoulders and the wet material stuck to her skin and the effort was futile.

"You're hurting me," she murmured.

The pressure did not ease and she felt that his fingers might penetrate the soft flesh of her shoulders. He just stood there holding her away from him and looking at her until she was overcome with shame and embarrassment.

"Let me go," she pleaded. Her anger was gone now and her former bravado had dissolved into fear. She wanted to run for the haven of her room and locked the doors, but his hold was not to be broken. The slightest move on her part, increased the already painful pressure.

"I'm sorry," she whispered. She could feel tears coming to her eyes and although his grip was hurting her, it was not because of the physical pain.

"Tell me the truth, Molly. I have to know. Did you mean what you said?" "A- about what?" She stammered and tried desperately to recall the words he had flung so carelessly in her rage.

"You know what I mean. Are you the vestal virgin that you appear to be, or the tramp that you just professed yourself to be."

She could feel the heat rising in her body and knew her face was showing it. But it was dark and she didn't think the telltale color would show.

"Well?" He demanded.

"I don't see why it matters to you." She tried to keep her voice steady but could feel the waiver in it. "I am only the housekeeper."

"Damn you, you just gone a bit too far."

He released her shoulders and swung her body up from the ground and into his arms. Before she could protest, he was headed for the open door to her room. This was the tall, fair figure of her dreams and for a second she wondered if she would wake and find that it had all been a bad dream. But the lights in her room showed her that the grimness of his expression was very real and a shiver of fear went through her.

"Please put me down, JC. I said I was sorry and I didn't mean what I said." Her voice sounded pathetic, even to her own years and she wished she could control it and sound cool and unafraid.

"You seem to be very good at playing games tonight, Molly. Shall we see who the winner of this one will be?" He did not put her down but continued through the door of her room, into the hall and up the stairs. She became very conscious of her nudity and the fact that she was completely alone with him in the house. He kicked open the door of his bedroom and striding to the bed, dumped her unceremoniously onto it. Her heart was beating hard and fast now and she didn't know what to do or say. When he went to the other side of the room and remove the phone from the book, she thought he was going to make a phone call, but he smiled ironically and said, "we don't want any interruptions this time do we, Molly."

She swung her legs quickly over the side of the bed and made a dash for the door. He caught her before she could get through into it. He turned her to face him and the naked desire was plain in his eyes. She was held by them as if by a magnet and only murmured a feeble, "no," before his lips were on hers. They were hard, but not hurting and her rigid form went limp in his arms as she surrendered to be in evitable. She did not protest his caresses, nor did she respond. She no longer felt the fear that had coursed through her body, but rather that she was in limbo and had as little control over her fate as she had over the form in her dreams. His caresses became more intimate and she felt her flesh respond, totally detached from her mind which seemed to float about her like a casual observer to the scene.

"Damn!" He uttered the curse bitterly and thrust her from him so abruptly that she almost fell. "Get the hell back to your room, Molly and stay away from me for a while."

She turned and walked silently from the room and down the stairs. She knew now that she wasn't a kid anymore and that she had a little more power over dates the then she thought she had. It should have made her feel better, maybe even a little smog, but it didn't. She showered and put on her 90 and sat in the velvet chair in the dark for a long time trying to sort out the feelings that he roused in her. The realization was long in coming, but when she discovered it, relief poured through her mind. She knew now the difference between love and lust. And that difference was very hard to see sometimes.

"Yes, Maria, I do love him," she said softly. She had loved him even when he was angry and she feared what he would do. When her fate was in his hands, she was willing to let him do as he would with her. His actions were not loving ones, but angry and lustful, and she was not able to respond the way he wanted her to. She was sure that he was very experienced with women and he knew the difference in her between last night and tonight. She knew, somehow, that he had never had a less than cooperative partner and would not force unwanted attentions on anyone, including herself.

She decided that she had made enough discoveries on her way to womanhood for one night, and went to bed. She would leave the future to fate.

Her tall, fair captor was angry tonight and when she would have quivered in fear before, she now felt kind of calmness that made his anger less terrible. It turned to a feeling of warmth and she found her head resting contentedly against his golden haired chest.

Molly rose at the usual hours the next morning, and although she felt a little trepidation at the thing JC, she was not as nervous and that she feared she could be. She started the coffee and mix the batter for blueberry pancakes. When he entered the kitchen she greeted him with the usual, "good morning, JC"

"good morning, Molly. What's for breakfast?" He sounded tired and she noticed that there were circles under his eyes.

"Blueberry pancakes."

"Sounds good."

She served him his coffee and put the batter on the grill. In a few minutes she placed a stack of fluffy pancakes in front of him and he poured syrup lavishly over them.

"Aren't you having any?"

"Yes, I'm cooking them now. Go ahead and eat, I'll join you as soon as they are ready."

She finished the cooking and sat down across from him. He looked up and seemed to be trying to read her face. She noticed that he not only had circles, but the whites of his eyes were red.

"The pancakes are delicious, Molly."

"Thank you."

They ate in silence and when he had finished, he pushed his plate aside. "I have my suitcase packed for overnight and have decided to leave for Boston right away. You can take care of the rest of the items we mentioned for my grandmother's room. There's plenty of money in the household account, even to cover the cabinet for the television. I'll trust your judgment of what to buy. I'll call you tonight or early tomorrow and let you know what time to expect us."

Molly nodded. "I'll do my best to come up with something that won't make Joan cringe and I'll take care of the other items to. I shall have to stop by the house and make sure mom and the kids are all right. If you call and I'm not here, you might try there."

"Fine. I'm sure that I wrote the number in my book."

He collected his luggage and jacket from the hall and went out the door. It wasn't until he had driven off that Molly regretted not trying to explain some of her actions the night before. It would be a lot harder to do it with another person around, and she somehow felt that it was important for him to know that she did not expect him to take the entire blame for the scene between them last night. It was a missed opportunity to prove to him, in a small way, that she had taken a big step in the direction of becoming a woman. Then she remembered that he would be calling that night and decided to carefully compose her speech for then.

When the kitchen was tidy and his room was done, she went through the yellow pages of the phone book and began calling furniture stores in the nearest towns to them. There were three smaller towns in a 20 mile radius that had furniture stores and she made a list of the locations and the numbers. The second store had a unit that sounded promising and was only 10 miles away, so she decided to start with that one. She called the other two stores on the list and decided to make a trip there, only if the first one didn't pan out.

She called home. Her mother was still there and still in an optimistic mood about her father, so she headed out to do her errands in a lighthearted. The drive to the furniture store only 20 minutes and when she saw the black lacquer cabinet with the classic happenings design, she knew that she could no better. She go to bed when she found out the price, but knew that JC would approve of the design and craftsmanship and not consider it much to spend. And they said they would be happy to deliver it later that afternoon with no extra charge. She arranged for a time when she would be there, and went to do the other small errands that were on her list.

She finished her shopping and decided to stop by the salon to see if Myra would like to have lunch with her it seemed like years since they had talked and so much had happened. Myra was delighted with the suggestion and Molly chatted with some of the other girls and customers while she waited for Myra to be free.

They went to the Chinese restaurant. Myra was full of questions about Molly's father. Everyone had heard about his attempt on his own life and she wanted to know what was the truth and how much was rumor. Molly filled her in and then told her about the developments in her relationship with JC. She didn't tell her everything, but enough so that Myra, who was quite astute, got the picture.

"What are you going to do, Molly?"

"I don't know, Myra. I do know that as silly as it seems, I've fallen in love with him. And I realize that my chances of having anything more than an affair with a man like him aren't too great. I guess I'll have to decide in the next few weeks whether it's worth it to settle for that. His grandmother's being there will relieve some of the tension, and by the time she leaves, I should have things sorted out."

"I know how levelheaded you are about most things, Molly but you haven't had much experience with men. Believe me, it can get out of hand awfully easy, even when you have your mind made up that it won't."

"Molly, my girl, it's good to see you."

Tim Murphy had entered and spotted Molly while she was so earnestly engaged in conversation with Myra. "Hi, Tim."

"And who is this enchanting creature with you, if I may be so bold?" Tim was surveying Myra with the same analyzing look that he seemed to use on any one female.

"Tim Murphy, Myra Coolidge."

They exchanged greetings and Tim switched his eyes back to Molly. "Since the boss is away, will you be free tonight? I'm still waiting to have that rain check claimed."

"I'm afraid I'm not Tim. JC will be calling tonight to let me know what further arrangements he wants made for his grandmother and I have to be there."

"How about after he calls? We could go to the second show of a movie."

Molly shook her head. "Sometimes it's quite late when he calls."

Tim grinned, "well, I guess I'll have to keep on trying then. I'm glad to meet you, Miss Myra Coolidge."

When he was out of earshot, Myra asked, "who is that dreamboat and why aren't you interested?"

"He works for JC in the office here. I met him the other night when JC invited some guests for dinner. He seems real nice, but I obviously can't get too interested in him when I feel the way I do about his boss."

"Of course, you're right, Molly, but she is so much closer to our ages and maybe if you gave him a chance, he could make you forget JC."

"I don't think so, Myra, at least not right now. I'm sure he'd be fun to go out with, but right now I have too much else on my mind."

"Well, if you come up with any more spare men that look like that, you might send one or 2 My Way. My social life has been the pits since I broke up with Steve."

Molly smiled. "I'll keep that in mind, Myra."

She returned to the house and carefully arranged the things she had bought in the bedroom that JC's grandmother would be in. The delivery truck arrived with the cabinet and they not only placed it where she wanted it, but installed the television set that had arrived that morning inside it. She was even more pleased with her choice when she saw it in the room. It was a close match to the wardrobe and dresser and looked like a larger version of a commode with the television installed inside and the doors closed.

She went home and had a quick bite to eat with her family before returning to await JC's call. She was surprised when the phone rang at seven and it was him.

"Is everything taken care of, Molly?"

"Yes, I found the perfect cabinet and the television is all installed in it. All the odds in and are in the room and I'll just need to add flowers tomorrow."

"Fine. We plan to get started by noon, so you can expect us

between two and three."

"Very well, JC, I'll be waiting. And JC?"

"Yes, Molly?"

"About last night - I want to - "

"Not now, Molly," he interrupted sharply.

"Won't you just listen for a minute? It's important to me to have you here what I want to say."

"I can't discuss it now. When I get home will be better, I think. Good night, Molly."

Before she could protest further, he had hung up. Her disappointment turned to anger. He could have listened to her remarks that she had so carefully thought out. She knew that it would be easier to have said them to him tonight on the phone then with those eyes proving hers. She didn't know if she could say what she wanted to in another day or so, and she became quite cross with his dismissal.

She was still fuming inside when a car drove up and she saw Tim Murphy get out and come to the door. She opened it before he had time to push the button. "Tim, what are you doing here?"

"Well, since you said you had to sit around all evening waiting for a phone call, I decided to keep you company."

"JC called earlier than I expected. I just hung up in fact."

"Well, then, may I come in and keep you company, or will take me up on that movie?"

Molly wasn't too thrilled about either choice, but she knew that he would not be easy to get rid of." She remembered that JC had forbidden male visitors and she wondered if it included his own friends and employees. The question had not arisen but she didn't think that he would approve of her being in the house all evening alone with him. Besides, she was still quite put out with him and the thought of sitting here by herself with her anger all evening held little appeal.

"If you'll give me five minutes to fix my hair and makeup, I think I would enjoy seeing a movie. It's been ages since I've been to one."

"You got it, although there is absolutely nothing wrong with your looks right now."

"Thank you. I'll just be a minute. Go into the living room and pour a drink if you like."

"No, I'll just wait here patiently for you."

Molly was true to her word and only took a few minutes to spruce up. They got into his sports car and were off down the hill at a speed that Molly felt was a bit in prudent. But he seems to handle the little car expertly and she had no fear.

The movie was amusing and she found herself quite relaxed when they came out of the theater. He suggested coffee and a bite to eat and she agreed that would be nice. The conversation was Light and she found herself laughing at his jokes with an abandon that she had not thought possible. At 11 she suggested that it was time to get home as tomorrow would be a working day for both of them. When they arrived back at the house, he walked her to the door and she thanked him for a nice evening. He grinned. "I don't suppose I'm invited in for a night?"

She grinned back. "No, you're not."

He dropped a light kiss on her for head. "You're a treasure, Molly.."

"Thank you again for everything, Tim. You saved me from a long, lonely evening with a lot of things on my mind. It was nice to relax and laugh for a change."

"I'm always available, Molly. You know where to find me."

"Thanks, Tim."

He grinned again, "but don't think that I'll always take the first no for an answer."

Tim drove off down the hill, a little slower than before, and Molly went into the dark, empty house. She was undressing for bed when the phone in the front hall rang. She hurried to answer it, her heart in her throat. She feared that it was her mother and something had gone wrong with her father's progress. "Hello."

"Where in hell have you been?" It was JC's voice and the anger came through loud and clear.

"To a movie. I thought it would be all right since you had already called. I didn't expect you to call back."

"Obviously. When you didn't answer, I called your house and even the hospital."

"I'm sorry if I made you worried."

"I was a little concerned seeing as you are there alone and I knew that your father was in bad shape."

"I said I was sorry. It just seemed like the evening would be long and lonesome and when Tim—."

"Tim? You went out with Tim?"

Why had she let that slip out? He might not have questioned her about who she went with and she wouldn't have had to lie, just let him assume she had gone alone or with a girlfriend. But it was too late now and she realized that she had added fuel to an already raging fire. There was silence on the other end of the line and she could see in her mind the anger on his face, the fire in the blue – gray eyes.

"It's not what you think. I met him this noon at lunch and –"

"You met for lunch, too? "

"No, I didn't meet him for lunch. I had lunch with Myra and he happened to be eating in the same place."

"I called back because you seemed to have something urgent to say and I waited into my grandmother retired so that our conversation could be more private. It seems that I wasted my time and money."

"JC, please listen to me. I did want to say something that is important, at least it is to me. Last night, when I said what I did, when I acted the way I did, I only wanted to-."

"I think, Molly, that last night is best forgotten by both of us. I apologize for my actions, though I don't consider myself completely to blame. Nevertheless, I am old enough not to react the way I did."

"I don't blame you, JC. That's what I'm trying to say."

"Shall we call it even, then, and forget it?"

Frustration was raising havoc with Molly's plan to act calm, cool and mature and she lashed out at him, "go ahead and forget it then if you can." She broke into sobs and put the receiver down. When the phone rang again, a few minutes later, she continued to sob into her pillow. Finally the ringing stopped.

10 CHAPTER TEN

Lethargy filled at Molly's body and mind when she woke in the morning. She felt as if she had not rested at all and dragged herself from bed. She showered and dressed mechanically. In the kitchen she poured coffee and sat down to drink it. The hot liquid brought a little life back to her limbs, but her mind was fighting any attempt at getting her thoughts organized and directed toward preparing for meeting JC's grandmother and facing him.

She had looked forward to meeting the lady that had partially raised him, but now the joy was gone. She thought, almost with regret, of what her life had been like a couple of weeks ago, boring and physically demanding, but somehow safe and less stressful than what she found herself facing now. Her impetuousness at taking this job, which had seemed so ideal, had placed her in uncomfortable situations and she was unprepared to cope with it.

She finished her coffee and called her mother. She wished she could join in the enthusiasm that her mother was displaying this morning. Her father had met some people that were going to try to help him with his drinking problem and he seemed very receptive to their suggestions. They were all hoping that he would continue to try to help himself. Perhaps the near tragedy had served a purpose after all. Mrs. Stark was doing most of the talking and was more high-spirited than Molly could remember her being in a long, long time. She felt guilty that she could not share in her mother's joy more fully, but Mrs. Stark was so wrapped up in her own happiness that she did not seem to notice Molly's almost unconscious replies. She suggested that Molly might be able to visit him soon if this mood continued, and that they were hopeful of his coming home in a week.

When she had finished the conversation with her mother, she took a basket and went out to find flowers for the guest room. She knew there were violets at the edge of the trees and headed across the back lawn to find some. There were both purple and white ones and, as she picked them, she found herself at the edge of what had been her "private spot." It didn't seem like a haven anymore. JC had shared it with her and she didn't want that emotion filled memory to claim her right now. She turned and went back to the house. There were daisies in the little field behind the house she had shared with her family, and she would stop by there later to get some.

She arranged the flowers into shallow crystal bowls and put them in the room that awaited Mrs. Stark. She surveyed it, looking for any flaw that might be corrected, and decided that it would meet the scrutiny of anyone, even Joan's critical eye.

She did some food shopping and Maria helped her gather a large bunch of daisies, chattering like a magpie the whole time about a new boy she had met and how things were going to be better at home now that her father was so changed. Molly found it unnecessary to comment much, so wrapped up in her own affairs was her sister. She looked almost enviously at the bubbling teenager and wished that she could recapture the innocent joys of that period of her life, if only for a little while.

Food held no appeal, and she sipped a cup of tea while she arranged the daisies. The clock indicated two hours until the expected arrival and she wished that it would slow down. The flowers having been delivered to the bedroom, she changed to the light blue knit dress. She made sure that the tiny, open faced sandwiches and scones she had prepared were ready for a snack if JC and his grandmother wanted something to eat when they arrived. She would make fresh coffee and boiled water for tea just before two.

She surveyed herself in the mirror, and despite the careful makeup, she was totally dissatisfied with her appearance. Her eyes look dull, even with the eye shadow and mascara, and her mouth seemed to droop. She tried to smile, but it looked more like a grimace and didn't touch her eyes at all. With a sigh she turned away from her reflection. The sound of a car door closing, brought her out of her reverie. She dashed to the front door and, drawing herself up as straight and tall as she could, opened it.

JC was helping his guest from the car. Molly had seen her picture and expected the white hair and aristocratic features, but the height and carry edge of the older lady surprised her. The lavender suit flattered her hair and coloring and, if she had known her age, Molly would have assumed her to be a much younger lady. She wore medium-high heels and walked with the confidence of a much younger person.

Molly crossed the flagstone patio in extended her hand. Her eyes met a pair of blue – gray ones, not unlike JC's but somehow softer in their scrutiny.

"Welcome, Mrs. Stark. I'm Molly, the housekeeper."

A firm hand took her own and held it while she surveyed her much longer than was necessary, or so it seemed to Molly. The firm mouth widened in a smile and she said, "thank you, Molly, I'm sure we'll get very well acquainted in the next few weeks."

JC was removing an enormous amount of luggage from the trunk and Molly turned to him. "Can I help take some of that in?"

His attention never wavered from the job he was doing. "No, thank you, Molly. Please take my grandmother inside and make her comfortable and I will take these upstairs. Perhaps you can help her unpack a little later."

"Of course." She turned back to the lady who stood there observing the two of them with assessing eyes and she felt herself flush. "Let's go inside, Mrs. Stark. I'm sure that you could use a cup of coffee or tea and something to eat."

"We had lunch just before we left, so I'm really not hungry, but a cup of tea sounds wonderful."

Molly led the way into the house and Mrs. Stark followed her into the living room. When she was seated comfortably on one of the sofas, Molly excused herself to get the T. JC was entering with the first load of luggage and Molly steeled herself for the remark that she feared he would throw in her direction, but his eyes just met hers briefly, coldly, and the message in them was more potent than any words that he might have spoken.

She hurried into the kitchen and made the T, arrange some of the food had so carefully prepared, on a read at to her guest. Mrs. Stark surveyed the tray of goodies and decided that she could indulge in one of the phone, especially since there was raspberry jam to accompany it. Then she noticed that the tray held only one cup. "Are you going to join me, Molly? I really would like to get to know you since we will be spending so much time together, and there are lots of questions I want answered. John has not been much of a conversationalist and I'm rather tired of his yeses and noes."

"I will get some coffee for JC and me and be right back."

Molly filled two more cups and carried them carefully to the living room. She sat down on the sofa across from Mrs. Stark and was immediately engaged in conversation.

In a few minutes JC entered, having made three trips up the stairs with his grandmother's considerable amount of luggage. She tensed as he sat down on the sofa beside her facing his grandmother. She could feel the warmth of his body, even though a sizable space separated them. At least she didn't have to face him and feel like she was under a microscope. Mrs. Stark kept the conversation flowing and there was no need for Molly to turn and meet his eyes, which she could feel on her from time to time. Finally, JC suggested that his grandmother might like to see her room and start getting settled. She agreed that that would be nice and he led her upstairs while Molly cleaned up the remains of their refreshments.

She would have liked to see Mrs. Stark's and JC's reaction to the room she had so carefully prepared, but they had not invited her long and she knew that JC, at least, had put her firmly back in her position of hired help. And wasn't that what she wanted?

She busied herself in the kitchen and then set the table for dinner, putting the plates at either end of the table. When JC and her. When she thought there, he avoided his eyes leaving the already perfectly aware.

He didn't say anything for a few minutes and that Simon was loud in her ear. Finally he spoke in the detached, formal boys that held one at a distance. "My grandmother is changing and would like your assistance in unpacking and a half hour or so."

Molly kept adjusting the items on the table. "All right."

"Dinner will usually be at seven while she is here."

Molly nodded.

"Another thing, Molly. I know that I agreed to give you Wednesdays off when you were hired. Again, this week that would be rather awkward with my grandmother just arriving. I would appreciate it if you could arrange to work tomorrow and have some other day free."

"Yes, that's **all** right."

He waited, as if hoping that she would say more, but when she didn't, he turned and left the room.

Mrs. Stark greeted Molly enthusiastically when she knocked at her door at half hour later. They worked together unpacking and deciding on the best place for her things. Molly enjoyed hanging the lovely clothes and helping to arrange a few pictures and other personal items that she had brought. It took about an hour, and Mrs. Stark seemed reluctant to have her go when she said that she must get dinner started.

JC appeared in the doorway and suggested that his grandmother join him out by the pool. She agreed and Molly hurried back to the kitchen.

She saw little of JC in the next week and a half. He was almost always either out or entertaining his grandmother and Molly had the opportunity only to accept his orders or ask questions about household matters. She saw a great deal of his grandmother, though, and thoroughly enjoyed taking her where she wanted to go when JC was available. It was especially fun to take her to the quaint little shops where antiques were sold. These items were hard to find and very expensive in California, and Mrs. Stark was having a marvelous time finding treasures for herself and her friend. He found herself learning and acquiring and I for the nicest pieces of furniture and glassware and she decided that when she could afford it, he would start collecting some of the elegant pieces herself. She knew that he would have to start with small items, but that it should be a good investment as well as providing pleasure.

On the second Friday of Mrs. Stark's visit, JC announced that he would be having a dinner party on Saturday. Joan had come back from Europe and she wanted to introduce his grandmother to some of his friends. Molly gulped at the thought of a dinner for eight on such short notice, but she refused to give him any indication that it was too much for her to handle. Mrs. Stark did not miss the flash of panic that crossed Molly space, though, and she announced that she would love to make herself useful and help with the planning and arrangements. Molly looked her thanks and they both were startled when JC said sharply, "you are not here to take over Molly's job, grandmother. You have earned some years to relax and enjoy yourself."

Mrs. Stark recovered quickly. "Now, John, you know that I have no intention of interfering with the running of your house. Being a man, I assume you are unaware of the amount of time and work that a party like this involves. I know how capable Molly is, but in most households the lady of the house does the planning for the entertaining and doesn't expect the help to do any more than cook and serve. I am not senile and I will enjoy having something useful to do."

"Very well, if you feel that way. But I will not stand for you standing over a stove or tiring yourself so that you don't enjoyed the party."

"Cooking was never my forte. Molly is much better qualified to handle that and then I am, but I know what I like to eat and can help with the menu and table arrangements and the like."

"Then you go to it, and please see that Molly has something appropriate to wear while greeting the guests and serving."

Molly flushed and said, "I'm sure the pink silk dress will do nicely."

"No, you are not to wear that!" He almost barked at her and left the room.

Molly felt her color deepened and she started to retreat from the room also, but Mrs. Stark stopped her.

"Don't let him upset you, Molly. We have lots to do and we can get started right now."

Molly sank into the dining room chair next to her and they started planning the day. When they had finished, she had her self-confidence back and was even looking forward to producing a dinner that JC could not fault.

The dishes that Mrs. Stark had suggested were not beyond her capabilities and she made a shopping list while Mrs. Stark got ready to accompany her to the stores.

At noon they arrived home with all the necessary ingredients, even the wine that would be served with each course. They ate a lunch together in the kitchen, as JC had not returned.

"Now, Molly, I am going to make an appointment to have my hair done tomorrow afternoon and I will treat you to a new hairdo also."

"Oh, I couldn't. There will be so much to do and all."

"Nonsense, it's just what you need to perk you up for a long, tiring evening and I'm sure that you must know someone to call in and help with the final preparations."

He said that he felt her "I have a friend that would help, I think, and maybe mother could come if my father is still alright."

"Well, call them as soon as possible and if they can't comment, we'll find someone else."

"Myra is working now, but I'll call her at five. Mother will still be at the hospital."

"I have the guest list right here if you would care to see it. I know Joan, of course, but have not met the others."

Molly scanned the list and was surprised to see Tim Murphy's name there. JC had been so upset that she had assumed that he would not be welcome here on a social basis. The Eli's had been included and that made her feel better. They were so nice and would add an air of friendliness to her evening. Joan was there and Molly now knew her last name, Allard, which rang a bell. That was the name of one of the larger companies in the city. She wondered if she were of the same family. Dino was there, of course, and another name she did not recognize, Bronson James.

"I have met all of these people except Ms. Allard and Mr. James."

"Joan is such a lovely girl. I'm sure you'll like her Molly. I think of her as a granddaughter."

The remark stung Molly as sharply as if a needle had penetrated the sensitive flesh of her breast. She regained her composure and hope that Mrs. Stark hadn't noticed her silence.

"I'll spend the morning preparing the food, then, except what has to be done at the last minute, and plan to have a couple of free hours in the afternoon to take you to the hairdresser's."

"I talked to Joan on the phone last night and she suggested one that she uses. She said she was sure they would fit us and if I used her name. I'll call now."

Mrs. Stark went to make the call and Molly took care of the lunch dishes. Then she hurried upstairs to make JC's bed and pick up his clothes. Mrs. Stark insisted that she could do her own room with the Friday lady doing some of the cleaning, and the fact that she would be arising at a later hour then the rest of the house once she got settled into the routine and back to her late night movies on television.

Molly had dreaded entering his room ever since the

experience of that Sunday and she tried not to think about it. But the memories haunted her each time she went in to make his bed and she could feel his anger as he threw her on the bed and the memory of his eyes, cold with hate, brought tears to her eyes. She wiped them hastily and finished as quickly as possible.

They shopped for a dress for Molly that afternoon and Mrs. Stark made her try on dozens, it seemed, before they found the simple white one that was mid-calf length and cut in simple lines that flowed over her lithe body like a caress. The bodice was scoop necked and accented the proud breasts. A wide sash of deep turquoise hugged her slender waist and broke the stark purity of the white. Mrs. Stark nodded approval as Molly modeled it for her, and told the clerk that they would take it. Finding shoes that matched was difficult, but a bridal shop had a pair of satin ones that matched the sash and they bought those. Mrs. Stark insisted on paying for the items. She told Molly that since JC had ordered her to buy a new dress, he would reimburse her for it.

The new dress carefully put away, and supper cooking, Molly called Myra and asked for her to help the next night. She was available and would even come earlier if Molly needed her. The hair appointments were at two, so Molly asked her to come at four. Her mother said that she could come at six and that would be perfect for the last minute cooking, which she knew her mother would do superbly.

Molly ate her meals alone in the kitchen now, before or after she served JC and his grandmother. She didn't bother to eat much, her appetite seeming to have disappeared and there was no one to notice her lack of desire for food. When she occasionally felt a little faint, she grabbed a glass of juice and let it go at that. Sometimes, as she sat at the kitchen table, she pictured JC across from her in his terry robe, needing a shape, and she wished that those times would return.

She was up early Saturday morning and had done a great deal toward that night's party, before starting breakfast. The kitchen had been very much her private domain since Mrs. Stark had arrived, so she almost dropped the coffee pot when JC spoke. "Good morning, Molly. Grandmother seems to be sleeping a little later this morning, so I thought I'd have my breakfast out here. I hope she isn't doing too much and won't be tired out tonight."

"She'll be fine, I'm sure. She is a very energetic lady and seems to know her own limitations."

JC took his old place at the table and she served him coffee and juice before starting the scrambled eggs and toast. When they were ready, and she had placed them before him, he said "bring your food over and sit down."

"I already eight," she lied. "But I will have some coffee."

When she was seated, she waited for him to take the lead in the conversation. It was a while before he began. "Have you seen the guest list?"

"Yes, your grandmother showed it to me."

"I hope that you will use some discretion with Tim being here tonight and that you will make every attempt to be civil to Dena."

She flushed with the sick feeling of her that she felt that his remark. Another person seemed to be responding as she said, "I will make every effort to control myself and not embarrass you.

"Good. I do want to say that you did a good job in my grandmother's room. The television cabinet was an excellent choice."

"Thank you," she murmured. Any joy she might have felt at his praise was now overshadowed by the remark he had made previously. She refused to let him see how hurt she was, and after a minute or so she was able to tell him about the arrangements that they had made in what she felt was a creditable performance of coolness and detachment. His eyes sought hers questioningly a couple of times, but she managed to withdraw them before he could read anything there.

When Mrs. Stark appeared in the doorway, Molly sprang up in relief and said she'd have her breakfast ready right away. She decided that she would join them in the kitchen rather than eat alone in the dining room. JC had another cup of coffee and kept his grandmother company while she ate.

The Friday lady had stayed longer than usual and all the rooms were spotless. Molly went through the house and picked up the odd item that JC had left around, putting off going to his room until she was sure he had left the house. She spent as little time as possible there and then returned to the kitchen.

After lunch, Mrs. Stark and Molly chose the linens and dishes and set the dining room table. Molly would cut some roses from the garden later that afternoon. When everything was done to their mutual satisfaction, they headed for the beauty shop.

While her own hair was being done, Mrs. Stark gave careful supervision to the operator working on Molly. Her hair was left fairly long, but cut so that the end split back from her face in a natural frame. Then, since this was an evening party, Mrs. Stark decided that her hair should be pinned up to give a touch of maturity and elegance that would be fit the dress she was going to wear. Molly had never tried her hair in that style and was quite amazed at the poise it gave her young face.

Myra was waiting when they arrived back at the house and she bubbled with enthusiasm when she saw Molly's new hairstyle. "You look like Princess Grace," she bubbled and then greeted Mrs. Stark with equal warmth.

Mrs. Stark went to her room for a short nap and Myra and Molly worked and chattered busily in the kitchen. When her mother arrived at six, there was only the last minute cooking to do and she took over that chore with delight, enjoying working with the marvelous appliances at her disposal. The guests were to arrive about 730, so Molly left the kitchen to her mother and Myra and went to her room to get herself dressed. She was careful not to get the new hairdo wet in the shower. Although her eyes didn't sparkle, she looked with satisfaction at the sophisticated lady that faced her in the mirror. "I don't look a bit like a kid," she thought to herself.

JC and Mrs. Stark were in the living room. He raised his eyes as Molly entered and, although they seemed startled for a second, he spoke evenly and coolly, "you were right, grandmother, the dress is perfect for her-I don't know about white though."

The last remark was almost an afterthought and said so softly that Molly wondered if it were for her ears alone. She quickly turned her attention to Mrs. Stark looked almost regal in the royal blue satin with the elegant sapphire and diamond pendant the only ornament to break its simplicity. Matching earrings graced her ears and set off the white hair.

"Mrs. Stark, you look terrific," Molly said with genuine admiration. "You look like a queen."

"Thank you, Molly. Now let me look at you. Something is missing. Now let me think." She studied Molly for a few minutes and then said, "I know. The neckline of that dress screams for jewelry."

Molly shook her head. "I have nothing that would be appropriate to wear with this. Since I am not a guest or hostess,

I'm sure that I'm not expected to dress in the same manner as the rest."

"Nonsense, it behooves every woman to dress to her full potential and I hate to see a job go not quite finished. I feel like an artist that didn't quite finish the painting."

JC spoke then. "I think I know the piece you need to complete the portrait, grandmother. Do you remember the necklace my mother received from my father on their first anniversary. She wore it every anniversary after that."

"The aquamarine? Yes, I do remember it. Do you still have it John?"

"Of course. I would never part with anything like that. I'll get it."

"Oh, please, don't. I couldn't wear anything that valuable and—"

"you will wear it tonight to please my grandmother, Molly."

She knew better than to argue with that voice, so she waited uncomfortably for him to return. The large oval aquamarine was a deep turquoise, almost the color of her sash, and the white gold setting was studded with a frame of small diamonds. The jewel felt cool as it settled against her skin, just above the swell of her breasts and his hands were warm against her neck as he fastened the catch securely. She held herself rigid and did not breathe until he had finished and she could feel his touch no longer.

Mrs. Stark smiled in satisfactory. "That is perfect, John. I'm so glad that you thought of it."

The doorbell rang and Molly was relieved to escape his presence to answer it. She was delighted that the Eli's were the first to arrive, and she exchanged casual chatter as she took Marcia's purse and stole and put them in the hall closet.

She remained in the kitchen, near the door to watch for the arrival of the rest of the guests, and to keep an eye on the final dinner preparations. Dena was her usual, observant, critical self, but Molly refrained from uttering other than civilities and she seemed almost disgruntled that she could not report some sort of impropriety to JC.

Joan arrived next. She looked just like the photos Molly had seen of her. Somehow, Molly felt disappointed, as if she had half hoped that the cameras had flattered her. But they hadn't. She wore the same shade of rose that she had chosen for the bedroom and it held her perfect figure like the clasp of a lover. Rubies glowed from her ears and a narrow circle around her neck, and her black hair shone like a ravens wing. She smiled, exposing her model's teeth and said, "You must be Molly. JC told me about you. I'm so glad to meet you in person."

Molly wanted to dislike her as much as she did Dena, but found herself liking her immediately. No wonder JC loved her. She was beautiful and gracious and warm, and Molly and beat her like she had envied no one before.

JC appeared and they embraced each other while Molly, turned and hurried to the closet with Jones purse. She longed to stay in the darkness of the interior and not have to face them again, but JC was demanding her attention.

"Molly, come here please."

She returned to the foot of the stairway where he stood with Joan. "Yes, JC?"

"Joan and I need to have a few words alone. If any other guests arrive before we come down, would you please introduce them to grandmother and offer them drinks? I shouldn't be long."

"Of course."

Their voices were low as they ascended the staircase and she heard Jones soft, liquid laughed as they rounded the bend of the stairs and disappeared from sight. She thought she knew what those few words would be, and the tightness in her throat was painful.

She did not go back to the kitchen, but into the living room where she explained to the Eli's and Mrs. Stark that JC would be with them shortly and that she would be happy to freshen any drinks that needed it. Everyone said that they were all set and she went back to the front door. Tim's sports car was just pulling up and she noticed that he had an elderly gentleman with him. It must be Bronson James, she decided.

It was and Tim introduced Molly with a grin, but definitely acted more subdued than she had ever seen him before. He had not called her again after the movie, and she was relieved, but wondered at the reason. Was it her refusal to have him come in or did JC have something to do with it? Knowing Tim's persistence, it was almost certainly the latter.

Molly led them into the living room and introduced them to Mrs. Stark. They both knew the Eli's and Tim took Mr. James' drink order and filled glasses for both of them. Molly wanted to retreat to the kitchen, but Mrs. Stark patted the sofa beside her and said, "sit down, Molly, and rest a minute. I am sure the kitchen is in capable hands and Marcia and I want to ask about some of the area events that we aren't familiar with. She said she believes there are to be some crafts fairs and mineral shows and the like coming up soon. Do you know anything about them?"

"Yes, there are always that kind of thing in the summer at the state park. It's only a half hour or so away. I'm not sure of the dates, but I'll check on it tomorrow."

"Good, I think I would enjoy that kind of thing. I hope you do, too, because it seems like you're the one who will have to take me, unless my grandson can get away."

JC and Joan entered the room and Mrs. Stark's eyes lit with pleasure. She stood and went to meet the younger woman. They embraced warmly. Molly tried to slip away unnoticed, but JC caught her arm as she passed. She wanted to wrench herself from the grasp that seemed to burn her skin, but froze in her tracks and looked up at him.

"Thank you for attending to the guests. Give us 20 minutes to finish our drinks and then dinner can be served."

She nodded and tore her eyes from his. She moved to leave but instead of releasing her arm, he went with her. He guided her into the dining room where the soft light of the sparkling chandelier bounced its rays from the silver and crystal beneath it. "Everything looks fine, Molly. My grandmother will sit in her usual spot and act as hostess. The Eli's and Joan will sit to my right and Dena and Tim and Bronson to the left. Joan and Bronson are to be seated at the end nearest grandmother. Grandmother will signal you when each course should be served."

She nodded again.

"Are you feeling well, Molly? You're very quiet and now that I really look at you, you seem thinner and a little pale."

"I'm fine. I really should get back to the kitchen now and make sure everything will be ready on time."

He watched her go with a thoughtful look, then went back to join his guests.

Molly and Myra served the food and kept the wine glasses filled. Tim paid quite a lot of attention to Myra, his eyes sending silent messages, and Molly noticed that Myra was even more effervescent than usual. She didn't have to worry about Myra, though. She handled man like she handled everything else-with a lot of enthusiasm and an equal amount of common sense.

By the time the meal was finished and the guests had retired to the living room, Molly was quite tired and feeling the effects of the lack of sustenance that day. Her mother had finished the cooking and left to look in on her father when the dining room had been restored to order and one load of dishes was washing, they sat down at the table and had coffee.

"Tim seemed quite taken with you tonight, Myra. If he asks, shall I give him your number?"

"Are you sure you're not interested, Molly? You know I wouldn't want to infringe on your territory."

"He's all yours if you can get him."

"That sounds like a challenge and I like a good challenge now and then."

"I almost feel sorry for him, then," Molly smiled across at her friend.

"What about you and the boss, Molly. Has anything worked out?"

"I guess you could call that history, Myra."

"Do you still —"

"yes, I still do, but I seem to be not even interesting enough for him to want as a diversion anymore. Did you notice Joan?"

"The gorgeous brunette? Who could help but notice?"

"Well, that is where his heart is and who could blame him?"

"They do make an ideal couple, don't they?" She noticed the look that crossed Molly space and exclaimed, "Oh, Molly, how thoughtless of me!"

"It's all right, Myra. You're right. They are perfect for each other and I can't imagine him getting angry with her like he does with me."

"What are you going to do about the job, Molly?"

"I don't know. I'll stay on if he'll have me, at least until Mrs. Stark returns to California. She's talking of staying into the fall to enjoy the leaves and fresh air. After that I don't think I could stay, especially if he and Joan get married."

"That gives you time to look for another job. Maybe you can go back to school." These past few weeks to have that dream anymore, Myra. I could never fit into college life again. If I have the chance, I might take some night courses though."

Myra stayed until the last dish was put away and then managed to time her leaving perfectly with that of Tim Murphy and Bronson James. Molly saw them exchanging words outside the kitchen window and smiled to herself. Those two would make quite a pair, she decided. The other guests departed shortly, except for Joan, and Molly decided that she would go to her room and take care of the living room in the morning. The exhaustion that was claiming her made her feel quite faint and she never reached the bed that looked so inviting.

She heard her name being repeated over and over. It was the voice of the tall, fair figure in her dreams. She tried to answer, but every time she opened her mouth, nothing would come out. Warm, strong arms were holding her and she just wanted to rest her head against the golden haired chest and sleep, sleep, sleep.

But the voice was demanding and would not let her go. Resignedly she opened her eyes. The room was dim and they adjusted quickly to the subdued light. The arms, the warmth, became very real and she raised tentative eyes to his.

"Are you awake, Molly?"

She nodded.

"Thank goodness, you must have passed out. I came in and found you on the floor and I've been trying to get some response for several minutes. I knew you weren't feeling well."

"I'm alright now, JC. I'll go right to bed and be fine in the morning."

"I don't think so. Nor for the rest of the day either, by the looks of you."

"I was busy and I guess I forgot."

He stood with her still in his arms and went to the kitchen where he sat her in a chair and proceeded to make coffee and the sandwich. She watched in a kind of been used Hayes as he waited on her. Then he sat down across from her and said, "eat."

She didn't think she wanted food, just some sleep, but once she started, she found that she was quite hungry and a bit of strength seeped back into her limbs.

As soon as she had finished the sandwich, he placed a dessert left from dinner in front of her and would not listen to her protest that she didn't want it. When he was satisfied that every scrap had been eaten, he said, "I came to your room to tell you how pleased I was with the arrangements and work you did for dinner. I was also going to retrieve the necklace you're wearing."

Molly fingered the jewel. She had forgotten that she was wearing it. "Thank you for loaning it to me. I know it means a great deal to you." She fumbled with the class and he rose and went behind her to assist. His hands were warm and gentle and she longed to lay her head back and capture them, hold them against the sensitive skin. As if he sensed her mood, he released the chain, letting the pendant drop into the neckline of her dress and his soothing hands massaged her neck and shoulders. She was so tired and it felt so deliciously relaxing. He eased her back against him and she caught her breath as the warm fingers slowly slid between her breasts to retrieve the jewel. They lingered there a bit longer than necessary and she knew that she would not, could not protest anything that he might choose to do with her.

He knew it to and she was willing to go through anything that meant having his strong warmth this close a little while longer. He drew her to her feet and she managed to stand, swaying only slightly, but more from the sensations he was arousing in her than from the weakness and exhaustion she had felt before. It was a lazy, languid desire that sought to be led, like a blind person in strange surroundings. He held her gently and his kiss was soft and tender. She laid against him and wished that there was a way to capture this moment in time for ever. When he lifted his mouse from hers, she murmured a protest. He laughed softly and scooped her up in his arms, turning off the kitchen light as they went through the doorway.

He laid her gently on her bed in her arms clung around his neck, demanding him to kiss her again. He did, long and sweet. Then he gently disengaged her hands and stood looking down at her. His eyes pleaded and she whispered, "JC, don't go. Don't leave me."

His face look tortured for a moment then he smiled, "not tonight, Cinderella. The clock just struck 12."

He was gone and she had never felt so alone, so betrayed, in her life. The tears came and then sleep.

11 CHAPTER ELEVEN

When Molly went to the kitchen the next morning there was a note on the counter beside the coffee maker. It was addressed to her.

"Molly," it said. "Since IOU a day off, I decided that today would be a good choice. You need the rest and I will take grandmother out to brunch and out for dinner. I have been meaning to spend more time with her and have today free. Have a good day. JC."

Rest would be welcome, but it left her feeling at loose ends. She made coffee anyway thinking that JC would come in and have some even if he was taking his grandmother out. But she drank it alone. At 9:30 she went to her room and put on her jeans and a T-shirt. She would go home and spend the day with her family.

JC's car was still in the garage, so she knew he must still be in the house. She tried not to think about last night as she went down the drive and headed for home. She had so hoped that his grandmother's presence would make for an easy relationship with him, but she now realized that it could never be. If they had a house full of guests, the odd opportunity would present itself for them to be alone in there could be no easy peace between them.

Molly's mother was just getting ready to head for the hospital and she was especially excited because she was going to bring her husband home today Molly said, "I better not stay than. I'll start dinner for you. You can call me when you're ready to leave and I'll be gone when you get here.

Tears came to her mother's eyes. "Molly, he is so changed that I really think she'll be glad to see you."

"I don't dare take that chance, especially with this being his first day home, mom. Just give me a call and I'll be ready to go. When he's settled and seems ready, then I'll be happy to come back if he wants to see me."

Mrs. Stark nodded and told Molly what she had planned for dinner. Mike and Maria went with their mother and Molly stood alone in the kitchen feeling like she really didn't belong here anymore. She peeled potatoes and put the meat in the oven. Her father was fond of chocolate pudding, so she made some and whipped fresh cream to top it with.

When the phone rang, she expected it to be her mother calling to let her know that they were on their way. She was surprised when it was JC's voice, and not her mother's, that answered her.

"Molly, I'm really sorry to bother you when you need a rest and a day off, but grandmother has had an accident and we really could use your help."

"An accident? What happened, JC?"

"It's not a life or death matter, by any means, but she turned her ankle and fell on the stairs this morning. I am at the emergency room of the hospital. Her only injury is a rather serious and very painful sprained ankle. I'll be bringing her home as soon as they have bandaged it and I was wondering if you could come home soon to help out. She hasn't even had breakfast and she will not be walking for a while, I'm sure."

"Of course, I'll go right away. I would have been leaving soon anyway as my father is coming home this morning."

"I'm glad to hear that, Molly. I hope it will all work out."

"Me, too. I'll see you at the house then."

She arrived first and mixed up some fluffy omelettes. She heated croissant's in the microwave and got out Mrs. Stark's favorite raspberry jam.

When JC pulled up to the front door, she went out to meet them. Mrs. Stark was obviously still in some pain, but she tried to make light of the injury. JC carried her into the house while Molly followed carrying the crutches she would have to use for a while. When Mrs. Stark was deposited on the living room sofa with her leg propped up on cushions, Molly quickly finished the meal she was preparing and brought it into the living room. JC looked hungrily at the laden tray and snatched a croissant immediately. Molly directed him to move the table closer to the couch so that Mrs. Stark could reach and to get a chair or ottoman for himself. When she returned to the kitchen, they were eating and joking about what a difference and invalided in the house was going to make.

Tab Molly went to her room and changed the genes for a skirt. When she returned to the living room and get case. "Molly, grandmother is going to have a lot of trouble handling the crutches for a while. She certainly can't go up and down the stairs and I hate to confine her to one room. The best solution I can think of is to have her move into your room for a couple of weeks. That way she can get outside and have her meals with me with a minimum of movement."

"Of course, where do you want me to go?"

"I thought the room next to mine. It was planned for a lady and I think you would be comfortable there."

Molly did not think that sleeping in the room beside his would add up to much comfort. She did not voice her thoughts.

"As soon as I get the kitchen cleaned up, I'll move my things and bring hers down."

"I don't think she'll need everything at one time. If you would find out what she needs for today, then the rest can come later."

When the kitchen was finished, Molly went to her room and packed the contents of her drawers in the battered suitcase. She gathered the clothes from her closet over her arm and headed up the stairs. JC caught up with her at the bend in the stairs and took the armful of clothes from her. "My grandmother says that since you are giving up your room, you must she doesn't want you deprived of a television or anything."

"It's really quite all right. I'll be fine in the other room."

"Maybe grandmother is right, Molly. I think her room would be a better choice."

"Very well, whatever you say."

She put the suitcase down and he laid her close on the bed. He sat down on the edge of the bed and said, "you pack and I'll lug."

Molly knew where they had put the things she thought Mrs. Stark would need that day and the next, and she packed them neatly in one of the lovely blue leather cases.

"This should do for now, I can always run up and get the odd item that she wants."

JC nodded and picked up the case. "I'll take this down and let you to do the putting away."

"I have to get my shoes and some other things out of the room first. I'll get some bags from the kitchen and do it right away."

She followed him down the stairs and when she returned to her room, bags in hand, he had joined his grandmother. She stripped the room of her belongings and made two trips upstairs with them. Then she unpacked Mrs. Stark's belongings and put them in the drawers and closet. Her own things could wait until later, as dinner had to be started.

She had the refrigerator door open, trying to decide what to make, when JC came back to the kitchen. "Molly, since another of your days off has been spoiled and I don't know when you can have another with grandmother needing you, she has suggested that we enjoy the pool this afternoon, and send out for Chinese food for dinner."

Molly looked up in relief. "That sounds good to me."

Very well then, I will carry her out to the lounge and you can get on your suit and we'll just relax."

Molly headed automatically for her old room and then remembered that it was hers no longer. She swung around and went up the stairs to the marvelous room that she would be using for a while. She wondered if Joan had ever slept in it, or if she was the first. As she put on the bikini, she thought that she must shop for a new bathing suit. JC had paid her once and she would be having another check in a week. Even giving her mother the amount she was accustomed to doing, there would be some money left to shop for herself. A new bathing suit tops the list.

Mrs. Stark was resting on the lounge under the umbrella and seems to be as comfortable as one could be with a sprained ankle. She said that the pills the doctor had given her were helping a great deal.

JC and Molly swam and laid in the sun. When they were thirsty, Molly produced lemonade. It was a much more enjoyable afternoon then Molly would have had on her own, and she almost felt like part of the family again.

When the sun started to go down, JC took his grandmother

into the house and Molly went up to change. They decided on what they wanted from the Chinese restaurant and JC called in the order so it would be ready for him to pick up.

When the food arrived, Mrs. Stark tried out the crutches and, although shaky, managed with JC's help to get to the kitchen. They ate together at the kitchen table and Molly's appetite was better than it had been in some time.

Mrs. Stark turned to JC as they were sipping tea and said, "John, I do hope that you appreciate all the extra work and lack of free time that Molly has put in lately. Most help would have been long gone today, and if they had been here, they'd have suggested you hire a nurse. And as for giving up your room, they would probably suggest that you carry me around or leave me upstairs all the time."

JC looked at his grandmother and then at Molly. The blue-gray eyes seemed to deepen in color as they met hers and he held her gaze as he said, "oh, yes, grandmother, I appreciate Molly. And given time, I will find ways to show my appreciation."

"Mrs. Stark continued, seemingly oblivious to the silent communication that was taking place, "well, I certainly hope so. I might have a suggestion or to myself if you need some help."

His eyes still held Molly's with their magnetic power. "No, grandmother, I don't think I need any help with this."

The wave of warmth that was sweeping through her, made her lower her eyes, and she lifted the cup to her lips and took a sip of the hot tea to ease the dryness that she felt in her mouth and throat. When she felt she could speak without a telltale quaver in her voice, she said, "that really isn't necessary. JC pays me very well and there are lots of times when he is away that I don't have much to do at all. You couldn't help getting her, and I'm sure will be very little trouble. As for the room, I have never stayed in such elegant quarters in all my life before."

"Well, you are certainly the most refreshing young lady that I have met in a very long time. John has told me how you gave up school to help your family and I am reminded of the way things were when John's grandfather and I were first married. Those depression years were very hard on everyone, but we did manage to survive, and when our son was ready for college, we couldn't help him as much as we would've liked. Then all of a sudden the business florist and we were able to do many things that we never dreamed of. We were able to help our son get started in the business of his own and he prospered, though his life was all too short."

She stopped talking and seemed to be lost in memories and neither JC nor Molly spoke to break the thoughts she was reliving. Then she blinked her eyes and rejoined them, saying "I think my only regret is that I didn't have more children. But, I did have John to finish raising and that took a lot of the staying out of losing my son. Now let's get at those fortune cookies, shall we?"

A small bag of fortune cookies accompanied the meal they had ordered and JC doled out to to each of them. Mrs. Stark brokers open first and read aloud, "wise is the person who knows when to speak and when to be quiet." She chuckled. Maybe we should have read these earlier. She opened the second and red, "you will journey far for the good of your family."

She thought a minute and said, "well, I have journeyed far recently, but I wonder if this means making the return trip."

Both Molly and JC assured her that they were certain it meant her coming to visit, not leaving.

"You next, Molly," she said. Molly obediently opened the first cookie. "Luck is with you and yours," she said. "Oh, I do hope that one comes true for my family. It seems to have gotten a good start with my father coming home today."

The second cookie had two slips of paper in it. They read "love has many faces" and "you are wise to follow your heart." She read them silently and was enjoined immediately to share them, which she did, feeling somewhat flustered at the thought of the interpretation Mrs. Stark might offer.

But that lady nodded and said, "those are good observations for anyone to be reminded of from time to time. Now you, John."

JC opened the first cookie, read it silently and then aloud. "All's well that ends well." He did the same with the second, reading first and then sharing. "You will find your way though the path is dark." Then he folded the little slips and handed them to Molly. "Put these in your pocket," he said. "Before you go to bed, read them. It may help you to keep some perspective and revive your hopes about your family and the future."

Molly shelved the bits of paper into the pocket in her skirt. They discussed ways and means of getting Mrs. Stark around for some entertainment while her ankle healed. She vowed that she would master the crutches, if it was the last thing she ever did, and that there was no reason that she couldn't get to the hairdresser's and to stores as most of them had no stairs to climb. On her letter writing, she decided, and could do much of that at the table on the patio outside her room. They could also entertain, as that did not require much effort on her part that she could do from a chair or on the phone.

When she decided that it was time for her to retire, Molly went with her to get out the things she'd need and they decided that she could shower in the stall in Molly's bathroom if she wrapped a plastic bag around her bandage. There was a wall rail in the shower and she would be able to stand on one foot for the few minutes that it would take with Molly standing by to help.

When she was in bed and propped up so that she could see the television, Molly left her, promising to come back when she had unpacked her clothes and made some semblance of order to the room upstairs. "I'm sure that by then you may want a drink or the television turned off, and we mustn't forget to have you take another pill so the pain won't keep you awake."

Mrs. Stark nodded and said, "you go along dear. John pointed out that this phone is on a separate line and if I need anything before you come back, I'll dial the other line and let him answer it."

Molly hung the close that JC had left on the bed and put her other things away. They didn't seem to make much impact on the larger room with its vast amount of storage. She felt almost like she was staying in a hotel for a weekend. The night was warm and she opened the doors to the balcony to let in the fresh air. At least now she would be allowed to sleep with it open.

Finished, she returned to Mrs. Stark and got her some water and the pill which should help her sleep. The older lady declared that she had been through enough that day so that she was sleepy anyway and that Molly could turn off the television and the lights.

JC came in just as Molly was leaving the room.

"Are you sure that you will be all right, grandmother?"

"Quite sure. If I need you all call on the phone like you suggested."

He went to the bed and kissed her on the cheek. "You're quite a trooper, old girl. I'll be in bright and early in the morning, if you don't need me before then."

"I'll bet that Molly will be here first," she said.

Molly turned out the lights and they left her to her rest. JC said that he had some work to do in his den and Molly decided that she would go to bed.

As she undressed, she remembered the fortunes that JC had insisted she take and read again before she went to bed. She took them from the pocket of her skirt and laid them on the bedside table.

She had always admired the sunken tub in this bathroom and she was tired. The thought of a long, leisurely bubblebath to relax her seemed like the most luxurious thing in the world right now. She poured lots of the sweet smelling liquid into the tub and turned the water on full force. By the time she was ready to step into it, the tub was overflowing with billows of feathery bubbles. She stepped into the tub and eased her body slowly into the cloud of warmth until the frost hit her chin. This was pure heaven. A shower would have refreshed her, but the immersion in the fragrant, hot bath soothed and relaxed her until she found herself almost falling asleep.

Reluctantly she pulled herself up and get out of the tub. Bubbles still clung to her body, frosting her breasts and thighs. She dried herself slowly with the thick, soft towel and put on her 90. As she slid between the silk pink sheets, she remembered the fortunes, and propped herself on her elbow to read them from the light of the bedside table. "You will find your way though the path is dark," she read, and then the other. But when she thought she would read "all's well that ends well," it said instead, "life is a stairway with love at the top." She thought about the two messages for a minute and then reread them. She felt herself blushing. Was he referring to them both being upstairs now and the darkness of the hall that separated their rooms? Surely some message was intended or he would not have faked the second fortune. She turned off the light, and tried to sleep, but her mind decided to keep running, though her body demanded rest.

When she did fall asleep the tall, fair figure of her dreams stood at the top of a long staircase. He kept laughing at her while she struggled to climb the stairs with her leg in a cast on crutches that were much too long.

When she woke, her first thought was of Mrs. Stark. She dressed quickly and hurried downstairs. She didn't want to wake her up if she were still sleeping, so she opened the door and peeked in. Mrs. Stark was sitting up on the edge of the bed, so Molly opened the door wider and said, "I hope you got some sleep."

"Oh, yes, I did quite well. If you will help me to the bathroom, I'll be grateful. I'm going to practice with those crutches today and it should be no problem after this for me to at least get those few steps."

Molly did as she was asked and then made the bed. She helped Mrs. Stark into the chair and said that she would be back in a few minutes with coffee and something to eat.

JC was on his way down the stairs. She told him to keep his grandmother company while she made breakfast. He smiled and said, "grandmother was right. I was feeling very noble at being up and dressed at this hour, but you did beat me to it."

When she returned to the bedroom with the food, she found JC and Mrs. Stark had moved out to the table on the patio. They had decided to eat there. They told Molly to bring her own breakfast out and joined them.

JC left for the office earlier than usual and Molly got Mrs. Stark dressed and settled with stationery and her address book. She said that she would do some letter writing while Molly did the chores that needed doing. Later she would appreciate Molly support while she practiced on her crutches. Molly said that she would be back in an hour, and that she would only have to call if she needed anything.

She had just finished JC's room, when the phone rang. It was her mother. Mrs. Stark was so excited that she could hardly talk coherently. Her father had been asking about her and wanted to talk with her. Molly's first instinct was to go immediately, but then she remembered that she had and invalided in the house. "Gee, mom, I'd love to come right away but Mrs. Stark sprained her ankle yesterday and can't get around very well yet. JC is at the office and I can't leave. Tell dad I'm sure I can come this evening."

Her mother sounded disappointed but said, "of course, Molly. I understand and I'm sure that he will too."

Molly hung up, hoping that her mother was right.

Mrs. Stark did quite well with the crutches, and when JC came home late that afternoon she showed him the six or seven steps she could take without stopping to rest. He cautioned her about overdoing and said that the doctor would come to the house the next morning to check and re-bandaged the ankle.

They had dinner back in the dining room that night, and Molly felt quite lonesome as she picked at some food in the kitchen.

When dinner was over, she asked JC if she could go home as her father wanted to see her. She wouldn't stay long and would finish the cleaning up when she got back.

He looked at her dubiously. "Are you sure, Molly? I don't want you to have to go through any such trauma as before."

"I'm sure it's all right. He's not drinking now and has been sober for a couple of weeks. Mom called this morning and said he wanted me to come."

"I still feel uncomfortable about it, but if you think you'll be all right, then go ahead."

"Thank you. I'll be back within an hour or so."

"If you're not, I'll be more than a little concerned."

"If I'm going to be longer, I'll call."

He nodded, "yes, please do."

Molly wasn't sure what she would say when she got there. She guessed she'd just have to wait and see how he reacted.

Her mother took her to the living room where her father laid on the couch. He was very pale after the ordeal he had been through, and his face was quite gaunt. He smiled when he saw her and she went to the couch and kissed him. "I'm so glad you're better, dad," she said.

"Molly, it's good to see you. You look good."

"I've got a little color now, that's all that's different."

"It becomes you. How is your job going?"

"Fine, dad. JC's grandmother is visiting and she sprained her ankle, so I couldn't come earlier."

"That's what your mother said."

Molly stayed for half an hour and her father held her hand while he told her how sorry he was about what had happened between them. She assured him that she realized that he wasn't himself and he was forgiven. When Molly said that she must go, the family was all in good spirits and she felt like a huge load had been lifted from her shoulders.

Joan had arrived while she was gone. She was entertaining Mrs. Stark with anecdotes from her recent European trip. She had brought some lovely yellow roses for the invalided and Molly put them in a vase and placed them on the table in her room. She made coffee for them and then excused herself to clean up the rest of the dinner dishes.

JC followed her to the kitchen. "How was it, Molly?" He asked.

"It went very well. My father seemed to glad to see me and he was very apologetic about how he's been. I feel like a load has been lifted from my shoulders with everyone so happy right now."

"Good. I was so afraid that you would be let down."

"If he will just stay sober and get himself together again, then it will be just great for everybody."

"I know how you feel, Molly. You earned the right to a little joy from your family."

JC went back to join Joan and his grandmother and Molly finished in the kitchen. She went in to tell them that she would be up in her room when they needed her and Joan immediately asked, "up? I thought you had the room downstairs."

She did, but grandmother's accident necessitated a move." JC answered.

"She's in my room," said Mrs. Stark. "We just swapped places and I really like being down here where I can do for myself."

"The Rose room? Do you like it, Molly? That's my favorite."

"It's lovely. I understand that you decorated it."

"Yes, I did, and quite well if I do say so myself." JC laughed. "Molly and I added a writing table and television, but I think you will like the result."

"I'll check on it later and let you know."

Molly went upstairs and sat on the balcony, letting the evening breeze cool her skin and ruffle her hair. She thought about her father and was satisfied that she had said and done all she could to ease his mind about the unpleasant episode that had caused their estrangement. Then she thought about Joan and how lovely she was. She saw the three of them sitting in the living room and sharing a wealth of common experiences. She thought of JC and the way he could dictate her feelings, her moods, with a look or a word or a touch. She knew that he was affected by her some of the time, too, but she doubted that her power of attraction was other than what any man felt when he saw a pretty woman.

She heard Jones car start and went downstairs to help Mrs. Stark get ready for bed. That finished, she went to the kitchen for a snack and JC joined her, as he decided that he was hungry too.

They discussed her father and the possibilities that might lead to a job when he was physically able to work. He said that if things progressed well, he would see if he could do something to help in that line. She thanked him and said that she thought she go to bed. He thought that was a good idea for both of them and when he turned out the lights and followed her up the stairs, her heart beat at a faster pace.

When she reached the top of the stairs, she turned and said, "good night, JC."

He looked down at her, his eyes unreadable, and said, "good night Molly. Sleep well." His eyes held hers for a moment longer and then he turned and went to his room.

She did sleep that night, like she hadn't in a long time. The air was cooler and less humid than it had been in quite a while. The breeze drifted in from the open balcony door, lulling her to sleep.

She woke feeling refreshed and ready to face the day. The room was chilly and she got up to close the doors before she noticed that they were not open. She must have gotten up in the night and on it, but she couldn't remember it. She showered, dressed and was about to go down stairs, when she noticed a small box on the night table. She opened it with trembling hands. Inside was a black velvet case which contained a beautiful opal surrounded by tiny pearls and diamonds suspended on a delicate gold chain. She was too surprised to know how to react. Carefully removing it from its sat in bed, she carried it to the mirror and held it to her throat. The smooth, cool gem sent flashes of red fire as the light caught it and the little diamonds winked and sparkled in the early morning sun. She was reluctant to stop admiring it, but she put it carefully back in its case and went downstairs to Mrs. Stark.

She wondered who was responsible for the necklace. She knew that JC had to have put it there and was the one who had closed the doors to her room, but perhaps he had done the air and for his grandmother. She thought about him being in her room while she slept and flushed a little. Evidently he didn't think it was prudent to wake her, or maybe he didn't have any desire to.

Mrs. Stark was already up and delighted know and that she had managed to shower and dress without Molly's aid. She said that she had woken early and decided to do for herself. Then she asked, "did you like the necklace, Molly?"

"Oh, yes, it's lovely. But you really shouldn't have done it."

"My goodness, you deserve it and I didn't do it. John did. He showed it to Joan and me last night while you were gone and asked if we thought it was appropriate for you. I was delighted with his choice. Now you have a suitable jewel to wear with the white dress. It will look well with other things, to, because there are so many colors in it."

"It is beautiful and I love it."

"Be sure to let him know that, Molly. He agonized over making the selection and spent a long time finding the right thing."

"I will."

She hoped to thank him in the presence of his grandmother, but he came to the kitchen before going to join her, so she had to face him without the security of a third person. She turned from the stove where the scrambled eggs were cooking and, looking up to meet his questioning eyes, said, "thank you for the lovely necklace, JC. You really didn't have to do it, but I appreciate it very much. You couldn't have chosen anything I would like better."

"I hoped that you would like it, Molly. It's little enough to thank you for all you've done besides your regular job since you've been here. I wanted to give it to you personally last night, but by the time I got to it, you were sound asleep. I know how tired you bed and I couldn't bear to wake you."

"I wish you had," the words came out spontaneously and she felt the color rise as she thought how that must sound. She sought for a more appropriate reply and stumbled on, "I mean I am sorry that you couldn't have my proper thanks right away."

That remark only made things worse, she felt, and her color deepened. He looked down on her bent head and said, "and and I to be denied your proper thanks because I was compassionate enough not to wake you?"

"Oh, no, I do thank you."

He put his finger under her chin and coaxed her to raise her eyes to his. "One small kiss is all the payment I'm asking, Molly."

She decided to end the torment as soon as possible, since she knew he would not waver from his request. She raised herself on her toes and hastily pecked at his cheek. He laughed and pulled her close and the kiss that he demanded in payment was long and thorough."

Of burning odor penetrated the kneeling senses and she

gasped as his lips released hers, "the eggs are burning!"

His arm is released her and she grabbed the pan of brown, scorched food from the burner. He grinned. "I'll keep grandmother entertained and take out the coffee and juice while you make some more. I'll explain that it's my fault for the hold up."

Her hands shook as she made a fresh batch of scrambled eggs and browned some ham slices. The second batch turned out perfectly and she was quite calm when she took them into the dining room.

By Friday, Mrs. Stark was moving around the house quite well on the crutches and decided that it was time for her to venture out into the world again. She wanted her hair done and thought that she would like to have lunch away from the house. JC said that he would meet them for lunch if Molly could handle the beauty shop. They agreed to meet at 1230 at the restaurant where he and Molly had eaten a couple of times before. Molly was delighted to get out for more than the few minutes that she had been leaving Mrs. Stark for trips to the grocery store, and since she now had some money to spend, was eager to shop for a new bathing suit and some other items she needed.

When Mrs. Stark was in the hands of the beauty shop operators, Molly told her that she would return in an hour and set off shopping. She found a pale pink two-piece bathing suit with white cotton lace layered over the pink and a plain white silk blouse that would make a perfect background for her new necklace.

She returned at the end of the hour and got Mrs. Stark back into the car. JC was waiting for them at the door of the restaurant and he helped his grandmother into the cool interior. Molly followed and when she heard Myra's voice calling to her, she looked in that direction. Myra was in a side booth toward the back and was waving wildly to her. "Molly, it's been ages since I've seen you."

She went to the booth and was surprised to see that the dark head that sat across from her friend belongs to Tim Murphy.

He grinned and said, "hi, Molly. I'm afraid that I am the guilty party that has been monopolizing Myra's time."

She looked from one to the other as they exchanged very familiar glances. "I have been confined to the house pretty much. As you probably noticed, Mrs. Stark injured her ankle and this is her first outing. I'm glad you two are hitting it off so well. Call me when you have some free time, Myra and I'll fill you in on dad's progress and all."

"I heard that he's home and doing well. I'm so glad, Molly." Myra's eyes went from Molly to JC who had seeded his grandmother and was standing looking in their direction. Then they came back to Molly. They asked questions that she could not answer, even if they had been alone. She excused herself so that she wouldn't keep JC and Mrs. Stark waiting, and hurried to their table.

JC seeded her and said, "it would seem that your friend and Tim are seeing quite a lot of one another."

"I didn't know about it until just now, but it does seem like they have formed quite a friendship."

They ordered and Mrs. Stark asked Molly if she had found anything to suit her while she was shopping. Molly told her about the bathing suit and the blouse. She said she was eager to see them as soon as they got back home.

After lunch they went home and JC returned to the office. Molly put on the new suit and tried it out in the pool. Mrs. Stark said that it was very flattering and she had made an excellent choice. She also liked the blouse and said that Molly should wear it with the necklace that night. Molly hesitated and asked if that wasn't a little overdressed for serving a meal.

"Nonsense. The best way to thank someone for a gift is to let them see you wearing it. Joan is coming to dinner and I'm sure she would like to see how it looks on you to."

Molly thought that Joan would be other than thrilled but kept the thought to herself. "Very well, then, if you say so."

The only skirt that Molly owned that could be worn with the blouse and gem was the white pleated one. A soft, black suede belt and decided that it would do. She swept her hair up in the style she had worn for the dinner party. Her ears looked quite bare, but she knew that she could not wear costume jewelry with the lovely gem.

Joan arrived before dinner and joined JC and his grandmother in the living room. She looked lovelier than ever in the pearl gray, thin strapped, dress with appliqués of tulips in bright rose and black along the hem and bodice. Her only jewelry was the pair of Ruby earrings that she had worn for the dinner party. Molly felt quite colorless beside her.

She immediately noticed that Molly was wearing the opal and

seemed quite sincere when she said, "it's the perfect thing for you, Molly. I knew that JC had good taste, but he has really outdone himself this time."

Molly looked down at the pendant which glittered against her, halfway between her throat and the rise of her breasts.

"It is very beautiful and I am thrilled to have it, but I wish he hadn't done it."

Joan laughed, the lovely liquid laughed that sounded like water in a brook. "My goodness, Molly, he certainly can afford it and from what I've heard, you deserve it."

Molly served the meal, which they ate leisurely, and she knew that JC was following her with his eyes each time she left the room. She wished that she could read that inscrutable mind and then she wondered if she would like what she read if she could.

After dinner the three of them went out on the patio and Molly asked if she could go home for a while to visit her father. JC nodded and she assured them that she would not be long.

Molly had forgotten how much later the dinner hour was at JC's house compared with her own family's. It was after nine when she arrived at the house. Her father was happy to see her, but seemed quite tired, so she stayed only a few minutes. She wondered if Myra would be home. She doubted it, but drove by her house anyway, just in case.

Myra was just getting out of Tim's car. She pulled into the driveway in back of them and called to Myra.

"Hi, Molly, it's good to see you. Tim just picked me up at work. I have the night shift this week."

Molly knew that that meant going in to work at four-thirty and staying until nine.

"I just wanted to see you for a chat if you were free, but since you're not, will make it some other time."

"I'm dying to talk with you to, Molly. I have so much to tell you and I want to hear all about your life. But I have this awful headache and had to have Tim bring me home instead of going to the movie we planned to see. I have to work tomorrow, too. Since you left, Isadora has lost a couple other girls and she hasn't had much luck in keeping up with hiring. Consequently, the rest of us have had to pick up some extra hours. I'm going to bed and tried to get rid of the headache and be ready for tomorrow."

Tim got out of his car and joined them. "Hi, Molly. Nothing's wrong, I hope."

"Oh, no, I just left my father and thought I'd drop in on Myra if she was home. But it seems that she is ill, so I'll leave you to your good nights and head back to the hill."

Myra grinned, though she appeared in quite a bit of pain. We sent them for tonight, I think. Tim why don't you and Molly see that movie? I know you wanted to see it."

Tim looked at Molly, "sounds fine to me."

Molly shook her head. "I can't. I said that I wouldn't be gone for long."

"Well, let's go somewhere for a Sunday and coffee then. I want to know all you can tell me about this imp here." He grinned and ruffled Myra's hair.

"She wouldn't dare," she retorted, then added, "go ahead, Molly. You seem never to have a minute away from that house and with Tim in your company, I know he'll be safe from the other girls."

Myra went in and Tim and Molly agreed to meet at the small ice cream shop next to the theater.

They talked about Myra a great deal and Molly felt certain that Tim was roving I had been leashed, at least for the time being. They talked quite seriously about the job at the salon and about Tim's job with JC. Then Tim told her that he was pretty certain that JC was going to transfer him to a branch in a larger city in the southern part of the state. He was concerned that that could affect his relationship with Myra. Molly was sympathetic, but advised him that if they really cared about each other, the distance might strengthen their bond and if it didn't, then probably it was all for the better.

"So here you are! Your father appears to have changed considerably!" JC's voice was not loud, but it cut through the quiet little shop like a bayonet slashing through paper.

Tim jumped to his feet and Molly followed. "Oh, JC, I'm sorry. I didn't realize how late it was and –"

she didn't finish the sentence as he said coldly, "if you will tear yourself away from Tim, I'd appreciate if you would go back to the house and we'll discuss it there. I have been looking for you for some time and am not in a mood to have an audience."

Molly almost ran out of the ice cream shop to the car. She knew that JC would be right behind her and she was anxious to get the car in motion before he could catch up to her. Maybe by the time they got to the house he would have cooled off a little. And if Mrs. Stark was still up, he couldn't be quite as severe.

There was little traffic and she knew that the headlights behind her were his. If only he would let her talk first, she thought, everything would be all right. She wondered if he had said anything more to Tim after she had fled.

Before she was out of the car, is pulled into the garage beside her. She sat for a minute, breathing deeply and trying to prepare her defense. It didn't last long, as he yanked open the car door and pulled her out in one movement. He didn't say anything, just steered her through the breezeway and into the house with a grasp that bruised her arm. He did not stop in the kitchen, but propelled her up the stairs and down the hall to her room.

"Your grandmother," she murmured.

"My grandmother is asleep. I did not let her see my concern that you had not returned, as I didn't want her to worry."

"JC, if you would just let me explain –"

"Explain what, Molly, that you let me worry about what had happened at your house and that, when I called, your mother said you had left an hour before? I drove all before I finally spotted you are all on but not you. How many times you are not, Molly?"

"Never, it's not like that at all."

"It must be nice to have a friend that will act as a decoy and help you out."

Molly's fear turned to anger as he suggested he was lying that Myra was. Her free his face with a crack that he surprised him. Keep gas when she realized what he. "JC, I'm sorry, but you won't give me a chance to –"

his was the only thing he might have said. He grasped the opal and yanked it from her name, breaking the delicate game and hurting her neck. He tossed it across the room.

"Please, JC, please listen to me." But she knew that her pleading was falling on deaf ears.

She stood, unresisting, as he stripped the new silk blouse from her body. She knew she would never wear it again when she heard the fragile material tear under his impatient hands. Her skirt fell about her feet and the delicate, lacy underwear joined it.

The ringing of the phone seemed to bring him back to reality and he stood torn between picking it up and ignoring it.

Molly spoke in a whisper, "your grandmother –"

With a desperate look at her naked body, standing tall and proud, despite the onslaught of his anger, he stepped away and listed the receiver.

"Yes, grandmother. No, you didn't wake me up. I'll be right down." He hung up and, giving Molly a last derisive survey, strode out of the room.

Molly went to the corner where he had thrown the gem which had delighted her so much. But here alone. She knew that the mother thought about walking the door. He or she would have a key somewhere that if you really want to come in, wife, angrier than before. So she turned off the light and got in bed, naked body shivering slightly as it met the coolness of the satin. She lay there, rigid and waiting for his return.

She woke up and realized that some time had passed and he had not come. The clock said to and she wondered if his grandmother had had some real emergency. She heard no sound, but being at the opposite end of the house, one couldn't hear anything from the other side. She got out of bed and slipped on her robe. The hall was dark and she made her way cautiously to the head of the stairs. There was no sign of light downstairs, either. She went back to her room and stepped out onto the little balcony. He could see a faint ray of light on the flagstone below her and knew it was coming from JC's private retreat. He wasn't sleeping then, and she thought about what restless and agonizing thoughts must be keeping him awake. As she thought about him, a feeling of tenderness swept over her and she made a decision that she knew was not that of a child, but of a woman. He sat on top of the and watch the light that is slightly separate in the rate of, tell it. Then she stood and walked purposefully down the length of the French door that opened in his room.

12 CHAPTER TWELVE

He entered the room, but did not turn on the lights immediately. He removed his shirt and tossed it across the chair and then looked toward the open doors, as if surprised that they were open. She heard him catch his breath when he saw her standing there, her tall proud figure outlined by the waning moon, her bare skin glowing in its light.

He moved slowly toward her and she stepped forward to meet him. When their bodies were all but touching, she raised her arms and put them around his neck. He stood there, rigidly, as if wanting to reject her, but when she stood on tiptoe and pressed her parted lips to his sperm ones, she felt the tremor that went through him and his arms came around her and pulled her close against him. His hands began to move restlessly over her body as if he couldn't touch enough of her at one time and she felt the eighth of desire rise until she could hardly bear it.

Her lips caressed his chest, and her breasts tingled with the memory of his touch. When she thought that she would explode from the torment of desire, he swept her up in his arms, their lips still locked, and laid her on the bed. He broke the clasp of her arms about his neck and quickly removed the rest of the clothing that separated their burning bodies. Their legs intertwined as his lips found her thrusting breasts and she felt his throbbing arousal against her. His mouse sought her ear and he breathed against it, "welcome to the major leagues, Molly."

She was almost crazed with wanting him to possess her, and she pleaded softly for him to and the ecstatic agony that wracked her riding body. The pain of his possession claimed her momentarily and then she was lost in a world of sensations that she had never dreamed existed.

A languid piece claimed her body and she fell asleep with her cheek resting against the golden haired chest of the tall fair figure of her dreams. She hoped that she would never have to wake.

When her mind stirred, she stretched like a cat after a long nap, and slowly opened her eyes. She was startled for a minute when the brown and beige surroundings met her eyes instead of the rose and gray. Then last night flashed through her mind and her languid body warmed with the memory of the experience. JC was not in the room in the bathroom door stood ajar. She looked at the clock beside the bed and knew a flash of panic. It was 9 o'clock and she should have been up hours ago.

She jumped out of bed and ran down the hall to her room. She showered and dressed in record time and ran down the stairs. Mrs. Stark was sitting on the patio and when Molly emerged, she said, "I do hope you are feeling better, Molly. JC said you had a bad headache and he wanted you to sleep late."

Molly felt a blush coming. "I'm fine now. I guess I was more tired than I thought. I'll get your breakfast right away."

"Oh, JC made us some breakfast. It wasn't like your cooking, but it filled the stomach. Have something yourself and I'll finish these letters. Then maybe we can mail them."

"Is JC here?" Molly almost feared what the answer would be.

"No, he had to go into town for a while. He said he expected to be back for lunch."

Molly had a cup of coffee and thought about last night. She had been so sure of her decision at the time, but in the light of day, she wondered what JC thought. Would he assume that he now could have her whenever he desired? Would he want her at all, now that the challenge had been met? She was torn by unanswered questions, and she wished that she had someone to talk to. Myra would be working until two and there was no one else. With a sigh, she tried to stop thinking about it, but her mind would not obey.

When she went up to make the bed, she relived every passionate moment that they had shared, and she decided that no matter what happened, she would not regret the moments they had shared. No one could take that away from her and she knew, even if he didn't, that her motivation had been love and that it was right at the time and place.

JC arrived at noon and she found herself surprisingly calm at facing him. He handed her a small box when he found her alone in the kitchen and she flushed when she thought that it was another thank you gift. She didn't want to be thanked for last night in this way. It was almost like payment for services rendered. She put the box, unopened, on the counter and continued preparing lunch.

"Are you going to open it?"

"I don't want you to buy me any more things."

He picked up the box and opened it himself. He thrust it in front of her. It was the "pendant with a new chain, or the other one repaired, and she flushed again at the thoughts she had had.

"I am sorry about last night, Molly." He looked at her flushed face and the slightest of smiles crossed his lips. "Not about that, darling, but that I got so angry and did and said what I did. If you only knew how frantic I was when I thought that something had happened to you. And then when I saw you with Tim, I felt like all my worry was being thrown in my face."

"If only you had listened and believe me, JC."

"I know and I am sorry. I'm usually quite a coolheaded person and don't get rattled easily. Somehow, you have upset that equanimity, Molly."

"I'm sorry that I upset you."

Mrs. Stark appeared at the door on her crutches and they exchanged almost guilty glances.

"Well, John, are we going to have lunch today or are you going to keep Molly from her work the rest of the afternoon? She is going to take me downtown to mail some letters after lunch and I have a hankering to check out a shop or two that Joan told me about."

JC and his grandmother went to the dining room and Molly hastened to put their lunch in front of them.

Molly and Mrs. Stark spent the afternoon at the antique shops that she had found out about. One of them had quite a large selection of antique jewelry and when Molly admired it, Mrs. Stark insisted on buying her a pair of small sapphire and pearl earrings. They were screw backs but she said she knew that they could be made into pierced quite easily. They would leave them at the jewelers on the way home. She also bought a lovely garnet ring which she said would suit Joan perfectly and a cameo pin for herself.

Joan was at the house when they arrived. She and JC had been playing tennis and her lovely legs were shown off to perfection by the short pink tennis dress that she wore. She loved the ring that Mrs. Stark had bought for her and declared that it even fit perfectly. The candidate was admired by both Joan and JC and then he shifted his eyes to Molly.

"Did you find any treasures, Molly?" He asked.

Before she could answer, Mrs. Stark said, "as a matter of fact, John, I found the perfect earrings for her. Her ears are so small and delicate that most antiques would be overwhelming, but they had some sapphire and pearl ones that were perfect. Unfortunately, they had screw backs, but we left them at the jewelers to be changed."

JC nodded. "Then all the lovely ladies have baubles to please them."

JC, Joan and Mrs. Stark were attending a concert at the local opera house that night and Molly decided that she would visit home and take Mike and Maria to a movie. She had seen so little of them lately and she felt guilty. She told JC of her plans and he nodded thoughtfully. "If Joan hadn't made the plans for tonight and secured the tickets in advance, I'd have asked you to join us, Molly."

"I don't expect to be included in your social plans, JC."

"I think you might have enjoyed the music. I'll see you later then." She wondered what later meant.

Mike and Maria were delighted to have their sister's company for the evening. They saw a movie and had hamburgers afterward. Molly's father was up and about now and attending AA meetings regularly. Everyone seems to be happy and although she knew the money situation was still difficult, everyone was optimistic.

The house was empty and dark when she returns. She made coffee, in case they wanted some, and then went up to her room. She tried to find a television program of interest and then just settled for the company of the voices. She heard JC and his grandmother arrived and decided to go down and see if she was needed.

They were in the kitchen when she reached the foot of the stairs and she could hear JC saying, "Joan is going to have to set a date soon, grandmother. Putting it off is only making things worse."

"I know, John, and I talked to her about it the other day, without trying to interfere too much. She said that she needs a little more time."

"She's had a year."

Molly felt guilty, like in the eavesdropper, and she cleared her throat and stepped into the room. "Can I fix you a snack? The coffee is made if you'd like some."

"Just coffee is fine, Molly." JC said.

Molly got out the cops and when asked to join them, shook her head and said she'd had some not long before and didn't want to be kept awake. She noticed JC raise his brows slightly, but he said nothing and she went back up the stairs with a heart about as heavy as one could carry.

She decided that Monday would be a good time to start making inquiries about a new job. Even if Joan postponed the wedding for a while, she couldn't stay in the same house and pretend that she didn't care. Not after last night. She thought about Joan and JC sharing this room, and she suddenly hated it. The thought of them sharing the bed as intimately as she had shared his last night made her feel ill. She decided to take a bath in the sunken tub, but the luscious bubbles and hot water couldn't ease the pain that filled her.

JC came in a little later and found her there, bubbles up to her chin and tears pouring down her cheeks. He knelt beside the tub and concern filled his eyes. "Molly what's wrong?"

"N-nothing," she mumbled.

She did not protest when he pulled her from the cover of the frothy white foam and she stood before his appreciative gaze without flinching. She felt numb all over and as his fingers softly touched and burst the bubbles that still clung to her breasts, she watched mutely through tear blurred eyes. He carried her gently in his arms, almost like she were a baby. Her body was still dripping and she knew the water would stain the rose velvet spread, but she didn't protest when he laid her on it.

He sat on the edge of the bed and the blue-gray eyes probed hers for answers that she could not give him. Finally he spoke, slowly, as if searching for the right words. "I wanted to talk to you all day, Molly, about last night."

"It's all right," she said dully. "You don't have to feel guilty about anything. I knew what I was doing."

"I thought so at the time, Molly, but by the time I found out how innocent you really were, it was too late."

"If it hadn't been for a lot of interruptions, it would have happened sooner."

"Yes, it would have," he sighed. But not without me being there to talk with you later. I should have woken you this morning, but I knew if I did I'd-"

he didn't finish and she knew what he to have done. The numbness held her mind, but her body began to tingle under his eyes and she knew that it would respond traitorous lead if he so much as touched her. He raised his eyes back to hers. "I don't think you have any idea of the effect you have on me, Molly. I knew from the minute I saw you in your waitress uniform, giving me a dirty look when you thought I was a masher, that I had to know you better."

"Well, you certainly do know me better," she said with just a touch of sarcasm.

"I do and I don't, Molly. That's what bothers me. If I thought that what happened last night was going to cause you to reproach your self, I'd be most upset."

"Forget about last night, JC. I have."

A glint appeared in the blue-gray eyes and she realized too late that she had said the wrong thing. "Well then, Molly, let's give you a night that you will remember," he said. She knew that there was no turning back for either of them, and within a few minutes, the numbness she had felt was melting along with her lips and limbs. She responded to his every caress as a fine instrument to a Maestro and the bitter-sweet music filled her body, mind and soul. There was no pain this time and her body met his in anticipation of the crescendo that the increasing tempo of the music was rising two. When the moment came, the crashing of cymbals dominated the other instruments.

His arms still held her when she woke. She looked at his features, so much softer and more vulnerable in sleep, and her love for him made her ache. She tried to move without waking him, but the arms tightened even as he went on sleeping. She smiled sadly and spoke his name softly, "JC, I must get up. Your grandmother will be awake and wanting coffee."

"MMhmm," he still did not open his eyes.

"Please, JC, you can go on sleeping, but I must get up."

He opened his eyes slowly, as if he was afraid that he had been dreaming and didn't want to let go of the dream. Then he smiled lazily and said, "if you've already forgotten last night, I can refresh your memory."

She flushed. "JC, your grandmother, remember?"

"I'll bet grandmother would not want me disturbed if she knew what I—"

Molly slipped out of his grasp and ran into the bathroom.

She heard him laugh and call after her, "I would share your shower, Molly, but that would only lead to further delays, so I'll use my own."

She didn't remember much about getting breakfast, only that it seemed to turn out all right. She avoided JC's eyes knowing that they would cause her to suffuse with color. Mrs. Stark seemed oblivious to the electricity that was dancing around the room and chatted about the fact that she expected the doctor to give her permission the next day to start using her ankle again.

When Joan arrived and stayed for dinner, Molly felt like a traitor, talking with her in exchanging pleasantries. She thought her guilt must be written across her face and she avoided looking at JC, though she knew his eyes were on both of them. She wondered how he felt, watching his future wife and his mistress talking together. It didn't show if he didn't feel any qualms, and she became angry with him for being so dispassionate. Then she wondered how she expected him to act. Certainly he wasn't going to tell Joan about her.

She dreaded the thought of the night and bedtime, at the same time, a change of expectation was going through her body. What was she going to do? She knew that whatever resolve she made, it would evaporate if he chose to have it that way. She contemplated asking to sleep over at home, but thought it a rather obvious and cowardly suggestion that he would ridicule.

The problem was solved for her, when JC announced that he was leaving for Boston that night instead of waiting until morning. He usually spent at least two days a week there and with his grandmother injured, had put it off. She was doing nicely and he knew that she could manage with Molly's help. He would be away for a few days catching up. The late-night drive would be much easier than facing the commuter traffic in the morning, and he would be able to get an early start at the office.

Molly didn't know if she felt relieved or disappointed when he made the announcement. She packed the clothes he asked for and brought the suitcase down to the front hall. He kissed his grandmother goodbye and asked Molly to go into the kitchen for a few last minute instructions.

He gave her a list of phone numbers in case was needed and she nodded at the instructions about who could have them and who couldn't. Dena had not been in much evidence since Mrs. Stark and Joan had arrived and Molly no longer worried much about her calling.

"Any questions or requests, Molly?"

"No, everything seems quite clear."

"Does it? I hope so, Molly." He kissed her gently and held her close for a moment. "Take care of yourself and grandmother and I'll call you every night."

She nodded. He stood there a minute longer looking down at her, almost like he was waiting for her to say something. But the lump that filled her throat and the tears that she could feel coming, made her turn away, so he went out to the garage and she watched the headlights of his car cut through the darkness and disappear through the blur of tears in her eyes.

Monday was a rainy day and Molly and Mrs. Stark stayed in. The doctor came and said that Mrs. Stark could begin putting a little weight on the ankle, as long as she didn't overdo it. She started using one crutch instead of two and was pleased with how much faster and better she could get around. She insisted that Molly eat all her meals with her while JC was gone. She spent a long time reminiscing about his childhood, his parents and his brother. Molly did not like to seem too inquisitive, but the older lady seemed to welcome her questions.

When JC called that night, he spent several minutes talking with his grandmother and then she turned the phone over to Molly.

"He wants to talk to you, Molly."

"Hello, JC"

"Are you alone, darling?"

She blushed as she noticed Mrs. Stark's eyes on her. "No."

"I take it grandmother is staying right there."

"Yes."

"Then just listen. I have thought about nothing but you all day long and the thought of you being there tonight and me here is damn depressing. I had hoped to get through down here in only a couple of days, but I have a list of appointments that may take most of the week."

"Yes."

"Damn it, don't you care?"

"I don't know about that, JC, I'll see if I can find out."

"What the hell? - oh for grandmother's benefit? It had better be."

"Yes, everything is fine. I'll talk with you tomorrow."

Molly hung up and turned to Mrs. Stark. Shall we watch TV for a while and then I'll make us a snack?"

The older lady looked a little puzzled, but she agreed that would be a good idea and they went into her room to find a suitable program.

The next day, Molly made several calls to friends and acquaintances, but no promising leads for a new job were in the offing. When Mrs. Stark was on her own again, she would make some personal visits to a few places and see if she could come up with anything.

JC called that night after his grandmother had retired and she wondered if he had been that busy or if he had done it deliberately.

"Did it rain there all day, Molly?"

"No, only this morning. I took your grandmother out this afternoon to do some shopping. We picked up my earrings and they are lovely. It was very generous of her to buy them."

"She likes doing things like that for people she cares about, Molly. What did you say they were like?"

"They are sapphires and pearls and the most elegant earrings I have ever had, or hope to have."

"Do you miss me?"

"Of course," she wanted to add that she had missed him every time he had been away, even when she had just arrived.

"Molly, please don't make me do all the talking. Can't you say something that will brighten my day?"

She could say lots of things, like, "I am aching to be held in your arms right now," and, "the sound of your voice is stirring the passion that your hands do so well," but only managed, "I am looking forward to your return, JC."

The curse that met her ears let her know that that was not what he wanted to hear, "Damn it, Molly, I thought you'd grown up more than that these past few days!"

His reference to her naïveté made the hackles of her neck rise and she snapped, "I'm sorry if I don't know the proper phrases for a mistress to croon into the phone. I will read a couple of novels and bone up."

His anger came through loud and clear. "Do you know how lucky you are that I can't get my hands on you right now?" The tension was too much and Molly slammed down the receiver.

She regretted what she had said to him, but the bitterness of her situation was closing in on her and she was helpless to control her own fate. He that she would tell him, when the time came to leave, why she had to do what she was doing, and why she had acted the way she had. He would understand, because he was an understanding and compassionate person when he was not being antagonized by the attraction between them. If he felt one 10th of the love for Joan that she felt for him, he could not help but understand. She would go to him in the light of day when there was no one else around and she would tell him in her woman's voice and way, why she could not stay, though the thought of never seeing him again was more than she could stand to think about. Even an angry, accusing JC was better than no JC at all. But she would get over it in time, just as he had recovered from his brother's death. The sadness would always be there, but the pain would lessen.

She drifted off to sleep still picturing how she would face him with honesty. The tall, fair figure did not understand her though, and no matter how hard she tried to get him to let go, he kept pulling her back with a leash she was wearing around her neck. A fiery opal hung from the end of the leash.

Mrs. Stark kept her occupied the next day with errands and requests, as if she sensed Molly's uneasiness and thought that keeping her busy would help. It had not occurred to Molly before, but what if she had become pregnant from her nights with JC? It couldn't happen, she thought, it just couldn't. But she knew the possibility existed and the new fear only added to her distress.

When JC had not arrived by dinnertime, she steeled herself for the phone call that would be coming. He wanted to talk button. The call never came and she went up to her room knowing that sleep was but a futile dream. She decided that, although the night was chillier than it had been, along, energy expending swim was what she needed.

She put on the new pink suit and went downstairs as quietly as she could. She didn't want to disturb Mrs. Stark, who, she felt sure, would think a swim at this time of night in such chilly weather was unthinkable. She was relieved to see, as she slipped out the French door in the living room, that the drapes were polled in her room.

She eased into the water, welcoming its warmth after the brief exposure to the cool night air. She swam for what seemed an interminable amount of time, and still she knew she would not sleep. She decided to give up, go in and just sit there and stare at the television set in her room until sleep came. She huddled in the water for another few minutes, bracing herself for the shock of the cold air on her wet skin, when she heard a sound that must be a car door. It was late and she had the half sinking, half elated feeling that it couldn't be anyone but JC.

She pulled herself from the water, and involuntary shutter going through her as she met the air. It was even worse than she had thought it would be. Her robe was on the lounge at the other end of the pool and she wanted to waste no time in getting back to her room, so she darted across the lawn and into the living room door that she had left slightly ajar. With luck, JC would visit with his grandmother for a few minutes and she could slip upstairs unseen.

She peered cautiously into the lighted hallway, and seeing that it was clear, she sprang up the stairs, two at a time. She started for her room, just as he stepped out of it. She stood there, shivering with cold and dripping on the carpet. Their eyes met and she wanted so much to run into those warm arms and tell him how glad she was just to look at him again. But his mood was not one which allowed any such familiarity.

"My God, what ever possessed you to go swimming in this weather at this time of night!"

"I couldn't sleep."

"Join the crowd. I came up to give you this."

He had a flat jewel case in his hand and he extended it toward her. "I told you I didn't want you to buy me anything more." Her voice sounded pouty, even to her own ears.

"Take it. All mistresses are entitled to some baubles." He thrust the case into her hands and stormed downstairs.

She went into her room, throwing the blue velvet case into the same corner where her opal had landed. Then, still wearing the wet suit, she stepped out onto the balcony, welcoming the coldness on her burning skin and against her watering eyes. It was partly her fault, she had to admit to herself. She was the one who had thrown the term at him. Evidently his sensibilities did not let him think of her in those terms. After all, Mistress had the connotation of a long-term arrangement. A flame was more like what it was.

She felt quite stiff and numb with cold, before she went back into the room. Her wet body had left a mark on the velvet spread the other night and she deliberately added to it, by sitting on it with the wetsuit. He could buy a new one for the future Mrs. Stark, she thought. She thought about packing and leaving right then, but she knew he would stop her. Besides, her only means of transportation was a car that belonged to him. She could call her mother and have her calm, but the thought of how upset she would be by the call this late, ruled that out. She couldn't decide what she should do and then she thought of Myra. She dialed the number with fingers crossed, hoping Myra would answer the phone and not one of the numerous other family members. She was in luck.

"Myra, this is Molly."

"Molly, I've been dying to talk with you, but at this hour?"

"I know it's late and I hope I didn't wake anybody, but it's important, Myra. Is there any way that you could come and get me?"

"Now? But what is—"

"I'll tell you all about it later. Just say yes for now and I will forever be in your debt."

"Sure, Molly, if you say so, I'll come."

"Thank you. Now listen. Give me about half an hour and then meet me at the foot of the hill."

"Molly, this sounds serious. But I know you wouldn't ask if it wasn't necessary. A half hour at the foot of the hill. Got it."

Molly hung up the phone and put on her jeans and sweatshirt. She locked the door to the bedroom and went out onto the balcony. The drop would be about 10 feet and she thought and she should be able to dangle from the railing, cutting it to seven. Before she lost her nerve, she climbed over the rail and let herself hang for a minute. Then the cold and the metal cutting into her fingers made her let go and she fell in a heap on the edge of the grass. It took her a minute to get her breath. Then she stood and decided that she would be better off to circle the drive on the lawn near the woods. The grass was heavy with dew and she had very wet, cold feet before she had gone very far. She shivered and started to run. It was dark now, as clouds had drifted across the moon, and she stumbled a couple of times. She had just reached the driveway at the end where it joined the road, when a big dark figure wound up in front of her. She wanted to scream, but no sound would come.

"Molly, you silly little fool, don't you know that you can't leave me?"

"JC," her voice came in a whisper.

He picked her up and swung back to the house with his long stride. She didn't say anything, just lay limply in his arms and listened to the side of his heart against her ear.

When they entered the house, Mrs. Stark called from the kitchen, "Did you find her John?"

"Yes, grandmother, I have her right here."

"Well come out here and have some tea. She must be frozen."

He did not put her down, but proceeded out into the kitchen where his grandmother stood leaning on one crutch and pouring water into cups.

"Put her down at the table, John and get this into her. Then I'll leave you two silly geese to get things ironed out between you. You can handle that this time can't you, John?"

"I think so, grandmother."

"Myra!" Molly exclaimed as JC sat her on a chair. "Myra knows you're not coming, Molly."

"But how?"

"I'm afraid you forgot that the line in the bedroom is the same as mine in the den. I was going to make a call and when I heard you talking, I eavesdropped. I called Myra back and assured her that I would take care of you for tonight. Then I went to your room and found it locked. It took me a few minutes to figure out how you planned to get out, but when I did, I headed out after you."

"How did you know her number?"

"I didn't have to, Molly. The phone has an automatic redial for the last number called. I just pushed the button and had her on the line almost as soon as she hung up."

"Oh."

The hot tea was bringing some feeling back into Molly's body and she knew that the time had come for her to give her carefully prepared speech, if she were ever going to do it.

She drew in a long breath and began. "JC, the reason that I had to leave tonight is the way I feel about you. About us. I can't stay here and just drift in and out of your thoughts in your bed when I know where your heart and your future lies."

"What do you mean, Molly? Are you telling me that I am too old for you?"

"No. Surely you can see how impossible it will be for me to stay on when you and Joan get married."

"Joan and me? What are you talking about?"

"I'm not blind. You obviously adore each other and I overheard you and your grandmother discussing setting date."

"Molly, I think we had better back up and start from the beginning. Obviously you have misinterpreted a number of things and I have too."

Molly nodded in he continued. "Joan and my brother were childhood sweethearts. They planned to be married and take an extended trip around the world for their honeymoon. Joan was with Jeff on the mountain when he was killed. He lived long enough to make her promise him that she would see that his body was cremated and that she would take the trip that they had planned by herself. He told her that he would be with her wherever she went. She carried out his wishes, having just returned from the journey that they had planned. She seemed to find solace in continuing on and on and not returning to a place where they had been together. She finally was able to face the future and come home. The urn with his remains is still in of all awaiting burial, and we won't make the arrangements until she feels that she can be there and say a last farewell to his memory. I am anxious that my grandmother be here for the service and I had hoped that she would be ready when she came back to make the final gesture. She hasn't been able to make a commitment to the day and time as yet."

That explained a lot of things to Molly and she began to feel a glimmer of hope well up in her. "JC, if you don't intend to marry Joan, does that mean that the way you feel about me is not just as a --." She almost said mistress or playing and remembered how angry he had been.

"I have never thought of you as anything but a lovely girl that I could not keep myself from loving and wanting. I thought it very hard from time to time, but I have lost the battle."

"I know that I wouldn't be the person that you would want for a wife. You should have an educated lady with a similar background to yours."

His hand sought hers as it rested on the table. "The only reason I had for fighting it was that you were so young and I was almost afraid to care for you too much."

"Why, JC?"

"It seemed to me when my brother died, that I couldn't stand to lose another person who was as close to me as he and my parents had been. I wondered if I were some kind of a jinx. I couldn't help but have a little fear for your well-being if I became too involved with you. But love does not have a reasoning mind and when I thought I might lose you to Tim, I was crazy with jealousy. He was so much closer to your age and seems to have all the attributes that you would be looking for."

"I never cared about anyone else after I met you."

"Do you mean that, Molly?" His tone was pleading and she saw another JC, one who had been there all the time, just waiting to make himself known.

She nodded. "I knew I loved you after the first week. I tried to fight it, too, but knew long ago that there was never really any contest."

He stood and she rose and moved to meet him halfway. "Let's go upstairs, darling," he said. "I am going to hold you and kiss you and make up for all the lost time."

She gave him her hand and they climbed the stairs together. As they entered her room, she spotted the velvet jewel case in the corner and went over and picked it up. She opened the velvet lid and gazed at a string of glowing pearls with a large sapphire set in the middle. Slowly she turned to him, "oh, JC these are too good to give a mistress," she murmured.

"You're right, Molly. They are. But they are certainly just right for a wife."

The beautiful gems glowed up from the floor, as he swept her up in his arms and carry her to the bed. "What will your grandmother think, JC?"

"She'll be thrilled to help you plan the wedding and to finally have a granddaughter."

"But I mean--."

"If you mean about us tonight, she'll probably assume that I am making love to you and I wouldn't want to disappoint her, would you?"

"No," she murmured, "I wouldn't."

13 CHAPTER THIRTEEN

Mrs. Stark was excited and pleased when she was told the plan they had to marry. She immediately started talking about reception plan and getting busy on the guest list. Molly, who until that moment had been engrossed in the wonder of having her love for Casey returned, and thought about what a wedding is someone of his position would entail. She sat there quite overwhelmed as the two of them discussed should be invited and what the arraignment should be for having so many that would need in the house.

Then JC's face clouded over and he said, "I really don't feel that it would be appropriate for the wedding to take place until after we have had the funeral services for Jeff."

"My goodness, you know, John. But by the time we can put all these plans together, surely Joan will have agreed to a date. I'm sure that when she hears about your plans, she'll want to take care of it right away."

"I hope you're right, grandmother."

Molly toyed with her food, feeling uncomfortable and having lost some of the joy she had felt. This was the part of JC's life that she had never known and never would know and somehow she felt almost jealous of the brother that still held such a large part of his thoughts and heart.

As if sensing her discomfort, JC turned to her. "I'm sure you understand, don't you, Molly? This is a matter that has to be laid to rest before we can properly celebrate in the way that I wish for us to."

She nodded. "I think so, take the. I know how much your brother making you and that it will take a while for his memory to become less painful. Naturally I don't want to do anything that will make you feel that you have that memory."

"Thank you, darling. I knew you'd understand."

When he left for the office her gently and said, "I'll talk with you today and see if I can't crop her to make the final just first. When she hears about it, maybe she'll be happy enough for us to make the decision right away."

Molly did the chores with a lighter, happier heart than she had had in her memory. She wanted to call her family with the news, but have promised JC that she would wait until they could go to the house and make the announcement together.

JC came home for lunch. He seemed quite preoccupied and not at all the happy lover that Molly expected. She was a little hurt at the perfunctory pack he gave her when she met him at the door and wondered if the newness of their love had worn off for him in just one day.

As his fiancée, he and Mrs. Stark announce that Molly must join them in the dining room for meals. She sat quietly while Mrs. Stark went on about who she thought they should invite and noticed that JC was only nodding and answering in monosyllables. She became more and more on EZ and was certain that something was wrong.

Finally Mrs. Stark asked, "have you talked to Joan yet, John?"

"He raised his head quickly from the plate he had been studying. "Yes I talked with her this morning for a few minutes."

"Did she commit herself, now that she knows your plans?"

"Not exactly."

"Is that a yes or a no?"

JC pushed his chair back from the table. "I must get back to the office, I'm afraid. I'll talk to you tonight about it." Without a backward glance at either of them, he was gone.

"Well, what can the matter be?" Used Mrs. Stark. Molly just sat there numbly, feeling hurt and bewildered and wondering how her beautiful bubble had been burst so soon. It was after JC finally came home. You Molly quick, though kids and refused anything, asking where you might find his grandmother.

"She went to her room to write some letters, I think."

"Would you excuse us please, Molly. I have some things to discuss with her that I must do alone."

"Of course, I understand." But she didn't and she had stubble to give him a little smile.

He was with his grandmother for more than an hour and how she longed to know what was being said behind the closed the door. When at last he emerged, he asked her to fix him some coffee and a light lunch. While she worked, he remarked on her new outfit and asked what else they had bought. She told him and wished that he would say what he had on his mind and stop this idle chatter.

He sat down across from him with a cup of coffee and decided that she could not stand the suspense any longer. "What's wrong, JC?"

His eyes met hers and she tried to read beyond the words he was saying. "If I thought it wise, Molly, I would tell you. I hope that it can be resolved soon. In the meantime, will it be too much to ask that you don't mention our engagement just yet?"

There was no answer in his eyes, just a kind of pleading that she would say she understood and asked no more questions.

She stared at the cup of coffee before her as if it were the most curious object that she had ever seen. Then she raised her eyes to his again. "All right, JC. If I am about to pledge myself to be your wife, I guess that I can do as you ask."

He relieved and his voice was almost tender, "thank you, Molly. I have decided that when I go to Boston next week, I will take you and grandmother with me. We can shop for a ring for you there where there is a larger selection and I'm sure you and grandmother can find ever so many nice clothes there."

"That sounds wonderful, JC I haven't been there since I was in college."

"You run along to bed now. I have a lot of things to get squared away."

She went to him and kissed him, hoping that his response would be one that promised more of the light later on, but his lips were almost cool and she felt disappointment knife through her.

She sat on the balcony and watched the sliver of light that escaped from his retreat for a long time. But finally she gave up and went to bed and fell asleep before it disappeared.

When he came down in the morning to find her at the stove preparing breakfast, he held her close for a minute, kissed her and then sat down in his usual chair at the table. She noticed that he looked like he hadn't slept much, if at all.

She took him his coffee, and laid her hand on his tousled head bent and kissed his cheek. "You look tired this morning, JC."

His hand captured hers and he squeezed it so tightly at her. "I didn't get much sleep, Molly. But don't fret. I've done with much less on other nights." He grinned wryly and she blushed.

Mrs. Stark joined them and they all were rather quiet while they ate. Then JC excused himself to leave for the office and Molly rather hoped that she could learn something from Mrs. Stark. She and JC's grandmother had become quite close this summer and she thought that there must be some kind of reassurance that the older lady might give her.

"Mrs. Stark, I know that something is wrong. I told JC that I would try to understand about not announcing our engagement right now and I'm trying very hard to understand the change in him, too. But how can I, when he won't tell me anything at all, not even a clue to what is wrong?"

"Molly, I wish that I could help you, but I am sworn to let John work this out himself." Mrs. Stark looked at Molly with worry and compassion in her eyes.

Molly rose and started gathering the breakfast dishes. Very well. I'll just have to be patient then, won't I?"

When the morning chores were finished, Molly went to the store for groceries and picked up some dry cleaning. Then on impulse, she decided to stop in and see JC at his office. She had never been there and it was about time she became familiar with his surroundings other than at home, if she were going to be his wife. She pulled into the parking lot of the bank and walked to the side door that led upstairs suite of offices.

And attractive girl with auburn hair and freckles was at the receptionist's desk and she smiled at Molly when she entered. "Good morning. May I help you?"

"I would like to see Mr. Stark, please."

"Do you have an appointment, Miss--?"

"No, I don't, but if—."

Before she could finish, Tim Murphy came through the door. "Molly, it's good to see you. Are you here to see John?"

The receptionist looked from one to the other of them and Tim grinned at her. "It's all right, Audrey. This is Molly Stark and she is the boss's housekeeper. I'm sure that he will want to see her." His eyes were thoughtful, questioning as he looked at Molly.

She realized that Myra must have told him about the other night and she was certain that he knew more than a little about her in JC, but not as much as he would have liked.

I've reinforced the intercom and she heard JC's voice. "Molly Stark here to see you, Mr. Stark," she said.

There was no reply and, for a moment, Molly thought that she was going to be rejected. Then JC appeared through the doorway on the left. "Molly, what are you doing here? Is something wrong?"

She wanted to say that there was and she would be grateful if you could give her a clue as to what it was, but she smiled up at him and said, "I was just out shopping and thought I'd drop in. I've never seen where you work before."

His expression was a mixture of relief and something else that she couldn't quite put her finger on. "Of course, Molly. I guess I didn't think you'd be very interested in where I spend my working hours. How about a quick tour and then I'll take you to lunch?"

"That sounds wonderful."

She followed JC through the door into a large office that contained four desks. Two were occupied and she smiled as she was greeted warmly by Steve Eli and Bronson James. She figured it one of the other desks was Tim's and asked JC who usually occupied the fourth. "That one is where our secretary, Jane, works. She is out today with a bad cold and we are having our hands full trying to operate smoothly without her."

He opened the door back, and she and his office. It was rather small, almost the size of his that will and she was quite surprised at how bare it was comparison. The desk dominating the room. A computer terminal sat on it and stacks of papers. Two large metal file cabinets were against one wall and a window in back of his desk looked out on the busy street. Too functional, rather than decorative, chairs were the only other furnishings.

"There isn't much to see, I'm afraid, Molly. I keep everything here playing and businesslike. Investors seem to have more confidence in a no-nonsense environment."

"That seems sensible, but it is very different than home."

"Well, if you've seen all you want to see, why don't we go out and have some lunch?"

"I should call your grandmother and tell her that I won't be there to fix hers. Do you think she'll mind?"

"I am sure that she will be delighted that you are having lunch with me and is quite capable of waiting on herself this once."

JC made the call and she knew that Mrs. Stark was telling him more than that it was all right that Molly wasn't going to be home for lunch. He listened for a few minutes without making any comment and Molly stood looking down at the busy street below, wishing that she could feel lighthearted and happy about this unexpected chance to have lunch along with AC.

They went to the Victorian house again and she remembered the wine and the rest of the day they had spent together after dining there before with nostalgia.

"We'll have just one glass of wine today, I think, since you will be driving."

He remembered, too, and Molly felt a sudden warmth that she had thought she was not going to feel again right off. She smiled and could feel the flush that interface with pink.

"You are looking lovely today, Molly. I like that outfit that you're wearing very much."

"Thank you. It's one of the new ones that you bought me."

Molly had liked this dress better than any of the purchases they had made. It was a sundress with diagonal stripes in blue, white and grass green. The snug bodice with narrow straps player below her narrow waist into graceful form and with the white slingback sandals with high heels made her feel tall and poised.

He didn't talk much during the meal and Molly noticed that he looked very tired. When they were finished, he took her back to the office parking lot, dropped a quick and quite unsatisfactory kiss on her lips, and she drove off in the little blue car with even more questions than she had had before bouncing around in her mind.

They had lingered over lunch and it was about 130. She decided that she had to talk to Myra and that she would kill the half hour until she got out of work looking for some inexpensive jewelry to complement some of her new sport outfit. She had noticed some silver and plated earrings in the jewelry store where they had had her antique earrings fit, and she went there to look.

She was the only customer and was receiving the undivided attention of the lady behind the counter, when the little bell on the door tinkled, signaling that someone else had entered. She didn't look up from the earrings she was trying to decide on until she heard the clerk say, "Ms. Allard, how nice to see you." And Mr. Stark called this morning to say you'd be in for the ring he left."

Molly turned, a smile ready for the always pleasant Joan.

But Joan was not the pleasant and charming lady that Molly had always known her to be. When she saw Molly, strange look crossed her face and she barely managed a "hello, Molly. What are you doing here?"

"I am trying to decide on a pair of silver earrings. Maybe you could help me make a decision."

"Ordinarily, I would, but I am in a hurry. Mrs. Gould, if I could have the ring please."

The clerk looked at Molly. "You won't mind if I get Ms. Allard's ring, will you? I'll only be a moment."

"Of course not."

Molly thought that now that they were alone, Joan might congratulate her on her engagement, or at least mention it, but she seemed nervous and tense and they only exchanged remarks about the weather and some of the jewelry on display.

Mrs. Gould returned with the required article and she opened the small velvet case to reveal one large, brilliant diamond set in prongs on the gold band. It shot fire in every direction and Molly gasped at the size and beauty of the stone.

"Do you want to try it on and make sure that it, Ms. Allard?"

Joan almost snapped, "no, just give it to me and I'll be on my way." She took the case, snapped it shut and wheeling around, left the store quickly. "Did you ever see such a lovely ring?" Asked Mrs. Gould.

"No, I never did ," Molly replied thoughtfully.

"I have no idea that it is to be an engagement ring. Mr. Stark brought it in and have it reset. He was quite adamant that it be done as quickly as possible."

Molly wondered what the effusive clerk would say if she knew that Molly, not the lady that had just left, was engaged to Mr. Stark.

She chose a pair of plain silver hoops, paid for them and left, even more questions than before adding to her uneasiness.

Myra was after two and she's particularly immediately. She climbed into the car and now that she had so much to tell and find out that they would need our together and why didn't they go home so she could change and then they could spend the remainder of the afternoon.

"Myra, I would love to, but I have been gone for a long time and there is dinner to fix. I just had to see you and confide some of the things that have been happening before I burst."

Myra took in the disturbed face beside her and said quietly, "my news will keep. Go ahead, Molly."

Molly filled her in on everything that she didn't know about the night that she had called for a ride. Then she told her how all of us sudden everything was changed, especially JC's attitude toward her and the plans they were to have made.

Myra was thoughtful. "It seems like the whole thing hinges on Joan, doesn't it?"

"It was after JC talked with her about setting a date for the memorial service that things seemed to go wrong."

"I think, Molly, that that lady is the problem and not just about the memorial service. Maybe she's decided that she wants a replacement for the one she lost. And what better one could she find then your boss?"

"Oh, Myra, I don't think so. JC explained all about how she and his brother were childhood sweethearts and the commitment that she had made to his memory."

"A year is a long time to hold onto something like that. She is probably ready to live again and I think that she had to move a little more quickly than she had planned when JC announced his plans to marry you."

Molly wanted to protest that she was wrong, but the events of the past couple of days did add up to something being more wrong than just a delay of the memorial service."

"Myra, I was just at the jewelers and while I was there Joan came in and picked up a ring that JC had left to be reset. She acted very strangely, not at all like her sociable charming self."

"Oh, Molly, I'm so sorry that all this has happened and just when you were so happy."

"So am I, Myra." Molly's voice sounded dead. "What am I going to do?"

"I wish I could help you, Molly. If there is anything that I can do, just let me know."

They had pulled into Myra's driveway and she got out of the car. It wasn't until Molly was almost home that she remembered that she hadn't even asked Myra how her relationship with Tim was developing.

She parked the car in the garage, surprised to see that JC's was in there already. She gathered up the bags in the trunk and went into the kitchen. There was no sign of JC or Mrs. Stark, so she put the food away and started the roast for dinner.

When JC entered the kitchen, she turned with a smile and raised her face to be kissed. But the expression on his face turned her smile to dismay and her waiting lips were never touched.

"Molly, please come into the living room. I have to talk to you."

"Could it wait? I'm in the process of getting dinner started."

"No, it can't wait." Silently she followed the tall figure into the living room. His shoulders slumped and he walked like a man going to the gallows. Her heart pounded with fear at the thought of what he was going to say to her. He stood by the fireplace and gestured for her to sit on the couch. She perched uneasily on the very edge and waited, half hoping, half fearing what he would say.

"Molly, this is the hardest thing that I have ever had to say to anyone. I had hoped that things would work out and that it wouldn't come to this, but my hands are tied and I have to do it."

Molly could almost feel the guillotine that was going to fall on her at any moment. She raised her eyes to his, almost pleading with him not to keep her hanging there any longer.

"Molly, I hope that you will understand and can someday forgive me. I wouldn't hurt you for the world if I could find any way to avoid it."

"Please, JC, just say what you have to say."

"I am going to marry Joan, Molly."

The guillotine fell and the pain was even more than she had anticipated. She didn't know how she could sit there and not scream or react at all. It was like she was disembodied in her conscious mind was watching a girl sitting calmly on a velvet sofa waiting for the tall man to continue.

"I have spent two days struggling with my conscience and with making the decision that I have now made. You are so young and I know that the her will be there for a while. But you will forget about me, Molly. I doubt that I can say the same for myself."

"I will get ready to leave right away, JC."

"Molly," he pleaded, "cry or react in some way, please."

Molly stood and her calmness surprised even herself, but how would she cry or react in any way when her head had been severed from her body and her heart had ceased to beat?

"I think it would be better for both of us if I pack and leave right now. I'll call my mother and have her pick me up. I know that she will be happy to have me come home again."

"Molly, you know that I will see that you and your family have enough money and I am working on a job for your father."

"We made out before I met you and I am sure that we can manage again. Thank you for the gesture, but it just wouldn't work. I gave my love freely and I don't want to cheapen it now with any offerings that you may hand out."

She turned and went up the stairs to the beautiful, hateful room. She couldn't stay here another night now that she knew that Joan and he would soon be sharing it. She put as many of her things in the old suitcase as she could fit and piled the rest on the bed. She went to the kitchen to find some boxes and bags. JC sat at the table, his head in his hands. But the two women in her own mind took over and she went to the laundry room to find the required items.

"Molly, at least let me take you home."

"I think that it would be better if you didn't. I know that the sooner I get away from the sight of you, the sooner I will recover."

Her mother didn't understand why she had to come for Molly immediately, but didn't insist on an explanation. Molly was relieved and when the shabby Chevy pulled up in front, she had all her belongings at the foot of the stairs. She had left the two jewelry cases on the Bureau in the room and all the clothes that he had bought her still hung in the closet.

She went to Mrs. Stark's door and knocked softly. When she heard her answer, she opened the door and went in. She had become very fond of the old lady and couldn't let her present situation stand in the way of saying goodbye.

"I've come to say goodbye, Mrs. Stark. I have so enjoyed knowing you and will treasure all the time that we spent together."

Tears misted the grandmother's eyes. "Oh, Molly, I am so sorry that things turned out the way they did for you. I had so hoped that John could - It doesn't matter now, I guess. Do you mind if I keep in touch with you? John has found another housekeeper, I know and I am sure that he will find no one as good as you. Perhaps we could go out for lunch before I go home?"

Molly nodded. "I would like to see you again any time that you want. But not here."

"What will you do now, Molly?"

"I'll find a job somewhere and get my family back on track. Things are much better at home now and I may even decide that I can leave and find a job somewhere else. I'll have to give it some thought first though."

"That is the best way. If you ever decide to come to California, please come to see me."

Molly nodded and dropped a light kiss on the lined chic.

When Molly went out, JC was engaged in conversation with her mother at the back of the car where they had stowed her belongings. She did not say anything, just slid into the passenger seat and stared straight ahead. She heard the trial close and then her mother got in and started the engine, which hesitated before turning over and finally came to life. She never looked back as they drove down the curving drive.

Mercifully, her mother did not talk as they drove the short distance home. Molly wondered how much JC had told her, but did not ask.

She was reminded of the phrase "you can't go home again" as she entered the house and it seemed like she was visiting, not returning as an occupant. Maria had moved into her old room when she had left and Molly insisted that she remain there. The little room that Maria had vacated, and which had its original purpose as a sewing room, would be fine she said. She took a long time unpacking, deferring facing her family as long as possible.

Mrs. Stark must have told them not to ask any questions, because everyone just made her feel welcome and chatted about plans that would involve her. She tried to join their conversation, but kept losing herself to the numbness that had set in, but which she knew was preferable to the pain that was bound to follow. She excused herself at 11 and went up to bed. She laid in the narrow bed and stared at the patterns of light that passing car headlights traced across the ceiling. In her mind she relived every moment that she had spent with JC, even the angry ones, and finally the pain welling up inside her became so intense that it sought relief in the silent tears that ran from the corners of her eyes into her ears and hair and onto the pillow. Then the great sobs came and wracked her body with their soul shaking depth. She thought that she would choke on the painful lump that had settled in her throat and refused to be dislodged.

She cried for a long time and did not remember when the sobs subsided and sleep came. She only remembered the tall, fair figure pushing her when she tried to get to the top of the staircase and the sound of laughter, like water over stones in a brook, that was coming from somewhere in back of him.

In the morning she woke, exhausted and drained of emotion, yet with a restlessness that would not let her remain in bed. She heard voices from downstairs and knew that the rest of the family was up and probably had been for some time. She showered and put on her most presentable cotton dress. She pinned her hair up in the style that seemed to add maturity to her young face and carefully applied makeup to the tier swollen eyes and face.

Then she went downstairs and faced the concerned looks of her parents and brother and sister. "Good morning, dear," her mother said, turning to face her from the pan she was tending on the stove.

"Good morning, mom. Is there any coffee?"

"Sit right down and I'll fix you some eggs."

"Just coffee, please. It's almost 9 and I am going out job hunting. I really don't want to take the time to eat."

"Molly, you really should. It will be a long time until lunch and you didn't eat any supper last night either."

Molly flushed as she remembered that she had been starting to cook it when JC had interrupted with the bolt of lightning that had reduced her palace and dreams to a mound of smoldering ashes. She wondered if anyone had bothered to finish cooking it or if they had eaten.

"I couldn't eat anything right now. I'll have something later."

"Where are you going, Molly?"

"Well, I can rule out musky's in the salon. But there are several restaurants and I even thought about trying to find a job outside of town."

"Whatever you think best, dear. But don't think that you have to rush, you know. Mr. Stark said that you have an account with quite a good sum of money in it and that he wants you to take your time deciding what to do."

"What are you talking about?"

"He told me that there is a checking account in your name and that he wanted you to use it until you got on your feet again.

"That was an account for the household expenses and it is his money and I will not touch it. I'll drop the checkbook I have off at his office today."

"Of course you know best, Molly, but he did say that you had some pay coming anyway and that he would deposit it in that account for you."

Molly finished her coffee and stood. "May I use the car for a couple of hours, mom? I can drop you off somewhere if you need to go to a job and pick you up later."

"No, it's all right. I will need it until this afternoon."

The car felt heavy and sluggish and awkward to Molly after this sleek little machine that she had become used to driving, and she decided that one of her priorities when she got a job would be acquiring a car of her own. It wouldn't compare with the sob, but she thought she could find something small and economical to drive that would give her more freedom than depending on the use of this one. She pulled into the parking lot of the bank and was relieved that the great Riviera was not there. She climbed the stairs to the office and was greeted by Audrey, who recognized her and said, "Mr. Stark is not in yet. Can I help you?"

"Please give him this when he comes in. I had intended to give it to him last night, but forgot." Molly handed the checkbook to the auburn haired girl and left before someone she knew came through the door and asked any questions. Halfway down the stairs, she remembered the set of car keys that were still in her purse and she turned and went back up.

Audrey looked up in surprise. "That was a short trip."

Molly flushed and put the keys on her desk. "Give him these two, please."

She was back in the car and out on the street just as she saw his car drive into the parking lot from the other entrance. Her heart beat a little faster as she noted the tall, straight form behind the wheel and she told herself that it was because she had had such a close call.

She returned home at noon, quite discouraged about the job situation. There were two restaurants that wanted her to come back as soon as their summer health left to go back to school, but no immediate openings. Her mother had lunch ready and she joined the family at the kitchen table. She ate a little salad but wasn't interested in much else.

"By the way, Molly, a Mr. Jonas called this morning and asked for you. He wanted to talk to you about a job, I think. I told him that I expected you this afternoon and he left a number to call after one."

"I don't know anyone by that name. Did he say where he is located?"

"I didn't catch all of it. I think he said some bank."

"Would it be the merchants bank?"

"I think that's it."

Then JC must have been busy this morning after she left the checkbook and keys. He wanted to be out of her life and he was going to be, completely. "Thanks, mom, but I don't think I'm interested in that kind of work."

"You are going to call and at least talk to him aren't you?"

"I'll think about it."

Mrs. Stark left just before one for cleaning job and Molly sat with her father and discussed the job that he had been interviewed for earlier in the week. It was a very small operation, but he would have a lot of responsibility and could work his way up quite rapidly he made good. He was very enthusiastic about the possibilities and Molly hoped that he would get the job.

When the phone rang, they both jumped up at the same time and then they both laughed. "You go, dad. I'm sure it must be for you."

Mr. Stark was on the phone for some time and when he returned to the kitchen, he was beaming. "I'm in, Molly! I start on Monday."

Molly hugged him, "I'm so glad. This will be like a whole new beginning for you and mom and the kids."

"And you to, Molly. If your mother keeps on working, we should be all caught up in a few months and you can go back to school."

She couldn't bear to put a damper on her father's hopes. "We'll see," she said softly.

Molly did not call Mr. Jonas. But he called her. He said that they had an opening for a teller and that they would train her on the computers.

"How did you get my name, Mr. Jonas?"

"From a colleague of mine."

"John Stark, perhaps?"

"Why, yes. He recommended you highly."

"I appreciate your offer, Mr. Jonas, but as I am not sure of my plans for staying in the area, I feel that you should give the opportunity to someone else. Thank you for considering me."

Before he could say anymore, Molly hung up. She went to her room and changed into her old jeans and then walked across the little field outback to the old sanctuary in the Pines. She waited for the peace that she used to find here to come over her, but it didn't. A few short weeks ago, the only dream that she wanted answered was that her father would snap out of his drinking and find a job. Now that dream was realized, but the one that had taken its place was smashed to bits about her. She wished that she had never met the tall, fair man with a magnetic eyes, had never known the heaven on his embrace and the shattering emotions that he could create in her. True, she had been only half living when she met him, but right now the saying "'tis better to have loved and lost" held no truth for her.

She stayed there, reliving the past few days, for a long time in when she felt that she could at least put on a mask of serenity, she returned to the house.

Her mother was home and she and her father were happily discussing his new job and making plans for the use of the car in mealtimes. When Molly entered, they looked almost guilty that they were so elated.

Molly decided that she needed a good dose of Myra and called to see if she were free that evening. Myra said that she had a date with Tim, but that they both wanted to see her and she should come with them to dinner and they would decide what to do after that.

"Oh, Myra, I don't know. I don't want to spoil your day and I don't know if I want to see Tim right now."

"Look, Molly, I know something big has happened. Tim told me that he has picked up bits and pieces. He's concerned about you, just like I am in the two of us see each other almost every day, so you're not breaking up any budding romance, for goodness sakes."

"All right. I need to talk to someone, and you've always been my best bet."

"We'll pick you up about seven then."

Molly told her parents that she would be going out for dinner and went up to change. She member, longingly, some of the new clothes that she had left behind, and then took out her denim skirt and top and got dressed. As she hung the gold chain around her neck, she saw a flash of fire and remember the opal. She wondered what he would do with it.

Tim's sports car pulled in promptly at seven and she squeezed into the minuscule backseat. His grand was the same, but his eyes were touched with sympathy and concern, as were Myra's.

"Hey, you two, you're supposed to cheer me up not act like this is a funeral."

"Sorry, Molly, but Tim has put in a wicked few days with your ex-boss and I am concerned about what I hear and the fact that you are working for him anymore when everything seemed to be ironed out the other night."

"I'm as confused as anybody, Myra."

Tim spoke then. "I don't know what has happened but I do know that John is the unhappiest, most vile tempered man I have ever seen. I know that he can get upset, but there is more to it than a simple misunderstanding this time, I'm sure."

Molly said "you remember what I told you yesterday? Well, JC not only was home when I got there, but he told me that he was going to marry Joan. So I and left and this time he didn't tried to stop me."

"What happened to make him change his mind overnight? He's not the fickle kind."

"I don't know, Tim. He didn't say. All he said was that he was going to marry Joan. I had run into her in the jewelry store that day picking up a diamond ring that he had left there to be reset."

"Probably your ring," said Myra bitterly.

"I don't think so. He said something about taking me to Boston to look for a ring. Of course, that was before the announcement about Joan."

"We did mention how perfect they were for one another, didn't we?" Myra said amusingly.

When they pulled and at the diamond club, Molly protested that she didn't think she was dressed for a place like that. They assured her that she was fine and they wanted to take her somewhere special to help her get her mind off her problems.

The restaurant was the most elegant that the small city boasted and Molly had been there only once before, on the night of the senior prom. The atmosphere was hushed and the lighting subdued. The floors were thickly carpeted and fresh flowers graced all the tables.

Tim had called ahead and when he gave his name to the waiter, they were ushered to a corner table immediately. Molly had little appetite, but she agreed to a glass of wine and they sat enjoying their drinks and discussing JC's puzzling actions. Molly felt better just sharing her bewilderment with them.

Then Myra said, "it seems like a mean thing to do, but Tim and I want you to be the first one to know about us. We had hoped that you could be as happy as we are, since you are the one responsible for us meeting in the first place."

"Mean?"

"Oh, Molly, you were going to get married and now you are and Tim and I are." The words came out in a gosh that Myra could no longer stem.

"I'm so happy for you both," and Molly was sincere. She loved Myra and had a great liking for Tim.

"We hoped you'd approve," Tim said with a ride grin. I never thought a couple of weeks ago that I would even be thinking about settling down for a long time, but I am going to be transferred to Nashua and the thought of only seeing this imp weekends was more than I could stand. Besides, if she would go out with a hopeless flirt like me, I knew it wouldn't be safe to leave her behind without a claim on her."

"Are you planning the wedding right away?"

Myra shook her head. "No, Tim is going to go in about a month. He'll need time to get settled in a new job with more responsibility. I need some time to save up for the kind of wedding we want and he can be looking for a place for us to live. Right now, we're thinking in terms of a Christmas wedding."

"That sounds delightful."

Tim grinned, "and at that time of year I can get away for a decent honeymoon."

Their food arrived and Molly made a pretense of eating, managing to force a little food down, but mostly just rearranging it on her plate. She glanced up in reply to a remark that Tim was making and her eyes froze. JC and Joan were being led this way by the waiter. They had not noticed her and she quickly dropped her head and toyed with her food while she sought some way to compose herself.

Myra did not miss the stricken look and her eyes sought the source. "Oh God," she breathed. I and said, "what is the matter? You both look like you seen a ghost."

Myra leaned closer and said quietly, "JC and Joan just came in and are sitting only two tables away. Why didn't we go to a pizza parlor?"

Tim looked at Molly. "We can leave if you like, Molly. Where almost finished anyway and we can have dessert somewhere else."

"No, I'm all right, and leaving now would be more obvious than sitting here pretending that I didn't notice them."

Molly tried not to look at them but her eyes were drawn like a magnet and she found herself meeting the astonished gray-blue ones. Their eyes held and there might not have been anyone else there for that few moments in time. Then he withdrew his eyes and the spell was broken, leaving Molly with shaking hands and a flushed face. Myra and Tim had not noticed the silent exchange, nor had Joan who was studying a menu. Molly was careful not to look that way again.

When they had sat for as long as they could over the remains of dessert, which Molly had refused, there was nothing to do but stand and make the most graceful exit possible. There was no way that they could pass the table and pretend that they hadn't seen its occupants, so Tim took the lead and said, "John what a coincidence that we should meet here."

"Yes, it is. Joan, you remember Myra don't you from the dinner party?"

Joan looked up at the three of them, and if she was surprised to see Molly, she didn't show it. "Hello, Molly, Tim. Yes, of course, I remember Myra." They stood for a moment, rather awkwardly, and then Tim said, "John, these quotes you wanted came in at the last minute this afternoon. I think you will be pleased and may want to act on them first thing in the morning.

"Would you excuse me for a minute"

"Of course, John."

JC stood and followed the three of them out to the lobby. Molly could feel his tall presence behind her and she had to force herself to move slowly and not break into a run. Tim paid the bill and told the girls to wait in the car and he would be right out. Then he and JC withdrew to a corner of the lobby and Myra and Molly went outside.

When they were in the car, Myra turned to Molly. "That was sure bad timing wasn't it? Who would dream that he would show up here tonight?"

"It's all right, Myra. It's not a very big town and I have to face the fact that I'm going to run into him now and then."

"Poor Molly, I wish that there was something I could do."

"Just be there to listen to me when I need it, Myra, like you always have."

Tim finally came out and got into the car. He had a grim look on his face and didn't speak until they were out on the road. Then he said, "John is leaving for Boston in the morning and is taking his grandmother with him he expects to be there for some time and he had a lot of instructions about the office."

"Is that all, Tim?" Myra asked. He glanced at her and shook his head. "No, darling, that isn't all."

"Are you going to keep me in suspense?"

"The message that I have is not for your ears, sweetheart. I can only give it to Molly."

"Oh."

When they arrived at Molly's house, Tim followed Molly up the steps while Myra got discreetly back in the car. She knew Tim would share the message with her later and try to help her figure out what to do about helping her friend Molly turned to face him. "Thanks, Tim. It was a nice dinner and it meant a lot to me to be able to share some of my problems with you and Myra."

"I don't think the dinner held much appeal for you, but we were glad to help in any way and we always will be. We both feel we owe you for helping us find each other and whenever you need us, just give a call."

"Thanks."

"John asked me to give you this. He was carrying it in his breast pocket and I think he has been for some time." He handed her a small velvet bag. "And he gave me a message to go with it."

Her hands clenched the bag and she could feel the hardness of the jewel through the soft cloth. She wanted to throw it, but decided she put it in the mail the next day instead. It was too valuable and beautiful to discard.

"He said, when, 'Tell Molly I love her'."

Tim didn't wait to see what her reaction would be, he just went back to the car and they drove off with Molly still standing on the porch holding the velvet bag.

She hardly heard the greetings that her family offered when she entered and, in a daze, went up to the tiny room that she now called hers. She sat in the dark on the bed and thought about what Tim had said. How could he love her and marry someone else? Was he only trying to soothe his own conscience over their affair, or was the message genuine in his decision to marry Joan for reasons other than love? And did it matter anymore with him committed to Joan that he did still care about her? Yes, it did matter. She had to know what she had shared with him was love and that she could remember with pride, not Shane, the complete surrender that she had made. With a sigh, she turned on the light and got ready for bed. The velvet bag lay there on the pillow where she had dropped it, and seeking to recapture just a little of the pleasure she had felt when she had first seen it, she opened the bag and drop the contents into her palm.

It was then that she realized how genuine the message he had sent was for in her palm rested, not the fiery opal, but the cool aquamarine with its circle of sparkling diamonds.

14 CHAPTER FOURTEEN

Summer and it and brisk, dry air of fall moved in. The leaves started to turn and as Molly walked along the sidewalk by the park and noticed the maples starting to catch fire, she remembered the Grove in back of JC's house and wondered if it would be as beautiful as she had imagined it would be. It seemed like everything triggered her memory of the first part of the summer and, although it caused pain, she found herself living more in that memory world than in the real one.

She had found a job that she liked working for a local newspaper. It was a small operation and she had to be a jack of all trades. Mostly she edited, but occasionally did some research and wrote articles for the Sunday edition. She was headed for the library now to find some information on a house of historical interest. Her hours **were** irregular and she always had to work late on Saturday night to get out the Sunday edition. But the lack of an opportunity for a social life suited her and kept the would-be matchmakers off her back.

Tim had been transferred to Nashua and she now spent a lot of her free time with Myra, helping her plan the wedding that was to take place just before Christmas.

She glanced up at the clock on City Hall and thought that she really must hurry and get her information. The library would be closing soon. She darted across the street just as a sleek gray car pulled out of the side street beside the library. The screech of hastily applied brakes startled her and she came out of her reverie to face the angry eyes of JC Stark.

"You little fool, I almost hit you!"

"Yes." The answer seemed very inadequate, but it was all that would come through her paralyzed lips. She had not seen or heard from JC since the night they had been at the same restaurant, and she was overcome with the emotion that his physical presence was arousing in her.

"Molly, are you all right?"

"No," she whispered.

He took her arm and led her to one of the benches in the park. She followed meekly, afraid to speak. She had thought to herself 1000 times how she would react when she saw him again, and she knew that it would be in inevitable that she would. But faced with the reality and without warning, she found herself speechless and with no defense at all. She sat there beside him and her eyes could not get enough of the sight of him. He seemed thinner and his hand was fading, but other than that he was the same JC that came to her in her dreams and who sometimes made her ecstatically happy and sometimes left her in tears.

His eyes were doing their own assessment of her and she knew that she looked like a lost weight, with her old jeans and sweatshirt and no makeup. "You are very thin, Molly," he said quietly

"Thin is in."

"Not that thin and you've lost your beautiful color. Have you been ill?"

"No, I've been fine. I work for the newspaper now."

"I know."

She raised her eyes to his questioningly and he continued, "you know that I had to be sure that you would be all right. I kept a check on you for a while to make sure you didn't go back to that Gresham fellow."

"I suppose Tim lets you know what you want to know."

"He is quite numb about you, actually, and I don't see quite as much of him since the transfer. It seems that he and Myra are getting married."

Molly nodded, "Yes, at Christmas time and I'm so happy for them."

"They do seem well suited and Tim, who always had a lot of potential in the investment business, is really doing well. I guess that he has settled down and decided to put his energy into making a good living for himself and his future family."

"How is your grandmother?"

"She decided not to stay as long as she had planned. I was in Boston for several weeks and she decided to go home rather than come back here."

"I'm sorry that I didn't get to say goodbye to her."

"Molly, there is so much that I want to say to you and I can't do it here. Will you come home with me?"

"Joan wouldn't like that."

A look of pain crossed his face. "Joan isn't there, Molly. She would never know."

"But I would know. Leave me alone with the memories that I have, JC. I am not ashamed of them and I would be if I let you make love to me again knowing about her."

"I only mean to talk, Molly. I know that I left you without any answers and that it was not fair to your or to me."

"If we were alone in that house, we wouldn't just talk no matter how good our intentions were. I don't want to tarnish what we had for so short a time. Leave me that, at least." Her voice was pleading because she knew that if he touched her or kissed her she would succumb to his wish without a second thought.

He stood, towering over her and looking down at her bent head he said, "All right, Molly. But someday I will find a time and place to make you listen. I hope that time is not so very far off. I trust that Tim gave you my message and the pendant?"

"Yes, he did, and thank you for that. It kept me from losing my self-respect. I know how much that pendant means to you, and I will return it. I meant to right away, but somehow I never got around to it."

"No, you may not return it. No one has ever worn it except my mother and you, and I don't intend that anyone else shall."

With that, he returned to his car and Molly sat on the bench long after the library had closed. The sun went down and the air became chilly, too chilly for the sweatshirt, but she still sat there lost in the world of what might have been.

Finally she roused herself and went back to the office. She told Ed Harrington, the editor in chief that she wasn't feeling very well and thought that she had better go home. She said she would write the article on her free day and he would have it for the Sunday edition. He nodded and told her that she was looking pale and that was probably the best thing to do.

She walked through the chilly night air without thinking about her destination and was surprised when she found herself at the shopping plaza that was just across the road from the street that led up the hill to JC's house. Consciously or unconsciously, it didn't really matter, her feet had headed in his direction without any guidance from her mind. She stood there for a few minutes and thought about going up that hill. It would be so easy to do. All she had to do was knock on the door and he would welcome her with no questions asked. A couple of tears trickled down her cheek as she turned and ran in the opposite direction.

She half hoped, half feared hearing from him again, but when the days turned into weeks and the weeks to months, she set the thought aside with the rest of the memories that she only pulled out now when she was alone and always the last thing at night before she went to sleep. Even the tall, fair figure of her dreams had seemed to find her company less interesting and she saw less and less of him.

By Thanksgiving, Myra was on needles and pins planning the final details of her wedding. She was getting so high strung that Molly took over being the advisor and spent a lot of time assuring her that everything would be perfect. She saw Tim only on weekends and he complained that he was getting damn tired of playing second fiddle to wedding plans and changes. Molly sympathized with them both and managed to keep their minor irritations from compounding into a real quarrel.

Her father was making great progress, both with his job and staying sober. He worked a lot of overtime and the family really had something to be thankful for on the holiday.

Molly took some of her carefully hoarded car money and did her Christmas shopping early. She knew that the last minute details of the wedding would require her services and since she was to be the maid of honor, she was giving a shower for Myra. That not only required a lot of time, but planning ahead and arranging for a time and place that would fit the schedule of the guest of honor as well as the important guests. Maria was thrilled when asked to help and she did much of the addressing of invitations and made some of the favors and decorations.

She bought her mother a dress that she would give to her before Christmas, as it was to be worn to the wedding. She chose it carefully for color and style and made sure that it would be appropriate for a number of other occasions too. She was very pleased with her selection and knew that her mother would look good in it. Mrs. Stark was working, but less than before and the lack of worry that she was now able to enjoy, had almost transformed her looks. She found a toolbox that her father had mentioned needing for work and she bought Maria the high leather boots that she had been drooling over all fall. Mike was harder, but when she saw the digital watch that was also a stopwatch and chronograph, she knew that he be delighted with it and bought that too.

By the time she had put on the shower, payed for her dress for the wedding and bought a wedding gift for Myra and Tim, the car fund was default. Oh well, there was always the new year.

The night before the wedding was rehearsal night and Molly met Tim and Myra at the church when she got out of work. She didn't have to dress for work, so had taken little interest in close or the way she looked most of the time. Myra looked at her in dismay. "Oh, Molly, could you have worn something a little dressier?" Should

"it's only the rehearsal, Myra. Tomorrow I will look gorgeous in my gown."

"But we're all going out to dinner afterwards and Tim's parents are doing the entertaining."

Molly looked down at her worn corduroy genes in dismay. "I'm sorry, Myra, I never gave it a thought when I went to work today. I'm sure that someone can run me home after the rehearsal to change. It won't take long."

"I guess that will have to do. Come on, we have to line up and get ready to march. The other girls are inside already."

They hurried inside and Molly took her place in front of Myra and in back of the other three bridesmaids, which included two of Myra's sisters and one of the girls from the salon. Tim hurried on into the church to take his place at the altar and gate get his instructions from the minister.

In a few minutes the music started and the girls in front of Molly moved one at a time at the proper intervals. Molly stepped forward and started the long march to the altar, listening carefully for the beat of the music and watching the backs of the girls ahead that she would not be going too fast or too slow. So intense was her concentration, that she had not looked at the altar itself. When she was but a few feet from it, she raised her eyes and stopped dead in her tracks. Beside Tim at the altar, stood JC. She had never bothered to ask about who the best man would be and now she knew. "Is something wrong, Molly?" Asked the minister.

She blinked her eyes and felt the wicked red flush sweep over her face. "No, nothing's wrong. I'm sorry to stop the proceedings. I'm sure I can do it properly tomorrow."

She hurried the last few feet and took her place, turning with the rest to watch Myra, on the arm of her father, make her way down the aisle. They all received instructions about standing, their duties during the ceremony and then it was time to march out. JC, as best man, would be escorting Molly up the aisle and she knew that that meant that he would be considered her escort through the reception as well.

He stepped forward and she took his arm. She hoped that her outward look was calm, because inside she was going to pieces. When they were all back in the vestry, Myra turned to Molly. "You are going home to change now, are you Molly?"

Molly could feel the color suffusing her cheeks again. "Yes, Myra, right away. I am sure that I can find something more appropriate to wear."

"I'll find someone to take you. Just a sec and I'll see if Jim is willing."

"Just a minute, Myra." When JC spoke, Myra turned with a start. "If Molly needs to go home to change, I'll be glad to take her."

"Oh, thank you, Mr. Stark, but I don't know –" Myra's voice trailed off as she looked at Molly, distress in her eyes.er

"It's all right, Myra. Go along and relax and enjoy yourself. JC and I will be joining the party in a few minutes."

Myra's relief at Molly's acceptance of the situation was as plain as the headline on the paper. She smiled her thanks and whirled off to join Tim.

"I guess you're stuck with me, like it or not."

"I'm sorry to have to bother you, but I wear old clothes at my job as it can get quite messy at times. I should have thought about tonight being special and come prepared. If you will just take me home and give me a few minutes, I'll make myself more presentable, though in what I don't know."

They went to the car and Molly remembered the first time that she had ridden in the sleek machine. It seemed like a long time ago, and she realized that it had been about five months. She leaned back against the soft leather seat. The moon roof was closed on this cold winter night, but she could see the sliver of a silver moon through the tinted glass of it. JC didn't talk and they were headed up a steep incline before Molly became conscious of the fact that they were not headed for her house at all, but for his.

She sat up abruptly. "JC we mustn't spoil the wedding supper. Please take me home and let me change so we can get there soon."

"It occurred to me, Molly, that most of your clothes are at my house. Since you were in a quandary over what to wear, I thought that you might well make use of what is there."

They approached the house and Molly was surprised to see that, not only were there several lights on in the house, but the windows glowed with the light of blue and white electric candles and garlands of greens were wound around the columns. An enormous wreath decorated the door and the whole picture was a giant Christmas card.

"Oh, JC, the house looks beautiful! Did you do all this or did Joan?"

"Grandmother is responsible. She decided that she needed to spend Christmas where there was snow instead of pam trees at least one more time before she died. So she is here for the holidays. Wait until you see the Christmas tree she made me put up in the living room."

Joan was apparently not here, or JC would never have brought her, and the thought of seeing Mrs. Stark again was appealing. So Molly got out of the car and went in with almost a feeling of homecoming.

Mrs. Stark sat in the living room before a roaring fire. The Christmas tree that stood in front of the window reached from floor to ceiling. She was sitting there as if lost in memories of past Christmases, when she became aware of Molly standing there. She blinked as if to clear her vision and then said, "Molly, it isn't a dream. You really are here."

Molly went to the old woman and kissed her fondly. "It's so good to see you again, Mrs. Stark."

"John, what a nice surprise! Is this my Christmas present?"

"No, Grandmother. You know what a stickler I am for making sure no gifts are opened until Christmas morning. I believe

I learned it from you."

Molly would have liked to have sat down and visited for a while, but she remembered the state of nerves that had overcome Myra and knew that she couldn't. "I'm sorry to rush off, Mrs. Stark, but we are expected at the wedding supper in a few minutes and I must change my clothes."

"Of course. I understand. But you will bring her back won't you, John?"

"I'll try, Grandmother."

Molly followed JC out of the room. "Where are the clothes JC?"

"In your room."

Molly headed for the door under the back of the staircase, but JC stopped her. "I said in your room, Molly. They are still hanging exactly the way that you left them."

"I don't understand. Where is your grandmother staying?"

"She's right where she was when you left and that's how she wants it."

"And Joan and you?"

"That is a matter that we don't have time for now. Get upstairs and change."

Molly hurried up the stairs, each step reminding her of the time she had spent in this house. At the end of the hall, she took a deep breath and entered the room that she hd promised herself she would never walk into again.

She turned on the light and her eyes widened in surprise. The same pale gray covered the walls and floor, but the velvet spread and curtains were in deep turquoise instead of rose. Then she remembered the stains that she had made on the spread and realized that of course he had replaced it.

She found the cocktail dress hanging where she had left it, the tags still on it. It was beige lace lined with aqua and she could wear the satin shoes that she had left behind with it. She changed quickly and swept her hair up. As she stood before the mirror, she noticed that the two velvet jewel cases still there, where she had left them months ago. Tentatively she reached for the smaller one and opened it to look at the opal she knew was inside. Surely she could wear it this one more time, and lie Cinderella, return it after the party.

JC said nothing when she descended the stairs, but his eyes

said a great deal. They said good night to Mrs. Stark and went out into the cold night air.

"You changed the color in the bedroom," she said.

"It needed changing and that color suited me at the time."

"I'm sorry about ruining the other spread."

"As I remember it, it wasn't entirely your fault."

She chose not to answer that and the arrived at the party a few minutes later.

Myra's eyes widened when she saw Molly. "Gee, Molly, you look like a bride-to-be yourself. What a gorgeous dress!"

"Thank you. It's just a little something that has been hanging around for a long time. I'll tell you about it sometime."

Molly and JC were seated at the head table, she to the left of Myra and he to the right of Tim, so conversation between them was impossible. They were served a lot of wine and some delicious food, which Molly found hard to swallow, so she concentrated on the wine. The party broke up at eleven with everyone instructed to go home and get a good night's rest and to be at the church on time.

"Molly, you can ride with Tim and me, " Myra said as they put on their coats.

"I think Molly will be riding with me." JC was in back of Myra and she turned to look at him and then back at Molly.

"It's all right, Myra. You and Tim go along. JC will take me home and I can return these to him tomorrow before the wedding."

Molly did not want Myra caught between the two of them the night before her wedding and she thought that she could handle any situation that might arise herself. She followed JC out to the car and, when they were seated, he turned to her. "I am going to take you home tonight, Molly, but I want one promise before I do."

"I guess that depends on what the promise is, JC."

"I want you to promise that when the wedding is over you will give me one hour with you alone to do the explaining that I need to do to you, and which I was not free to do before."

"Can any purpose be served by it now?"

"I hope so, Molly. Oh, how I hope so."

"If it's so important to you, then I guess that I can promise that."

"Thank you."

They drove the short distance to her house in silence., each lost in their own thoughts, but very conscious of the other. When they arrived at the house, all the lights were out except one left on in the kitchen for Molly. Molly reached behind her neck to remove the opal. JC watched what she was doing and said with a sigh, "That is yours, Molly, and I do wish that you would stop returning it. You could wear it tomorrow."

"My dress is deep red velvet and I'm afraid this is not the right thing to wear with it. I was hoping to wear blue and the aquamarine, but this is a Christmas wedding and Myra wanted red and green."

"You are quite an exasperating girl sometimes, Molly Stark."

But he leaned over and helped her unfasten the safety catch on the pendant, while she held her breath as his hands touched the nape of her neck. How she wished that they would stay there and caress her the way they used to do.

The necklace fell free and he slid it into his pocket. With a hasty, "Thanks for the ride and everything," Molly slid quickly out of the car and almost ran for the steps. He sat there and watched while she let herself in and then slowly backed the car out into the street.

The wedding was at eleven o'clock and the morning hours at the Stark household were quite frantic as everyone demanded equal bathroom time and the men had more things that they couldn't find than that they could. Molly dressed last as she did not want to risk crushing the velvet gown by sitting down once it was on. Riding to the church in the car with four other people would be bad enough without making any creases beforehand. She came down the stairs at ten-thirty to the admiration of her family. The low cut gown was edged with a band of soft white fur and her upswept hair emphasized the length of the graceful neck.

"Gee, Molly, you look like Snow White or Sleeping Beauty or somebody in one of the books I had when I was a kid," Mike said.

"And," said Maria, "your prince has just pulled in with his marvelous chariot."

"What do you mean?"

"Mr. Stark just drove in. Are you riding to the wedding with him?"

"That would solve the problem of crushing the dress," said

Mrs. Stark.

Maria opened the door and greeted JC, who looked like a prince indeed in his light gray tuxedo. He surveyed Molly and declared that she certainly did look fine, probably better than the bride.

"I thought it might be easier for you to ride with me than to crowd the car, Molly, and I am sure that Myra will feel better if we are there a little early."

Molly agreed and she put her coat over her bare shoulders to protect them from the cold, clear December air. They parked in front of the church in the spot that had been allocated to the wedding party, and when Molly would have gotten out of the car, JC's hand caught her arm.

"Grandmother asked what you were wearing, Molly. She sent this for you to wear." From his pocket he drew a deep red ruby on a fine white gold chain. "She said to remind you about unfinished paintings. Bronson is picking her up and escorting her to the wedding and I know she will feel hurt if you don't wear it."

Molly closed the mouth that had opened automatically in refusal and nodded. He put the jewel around her neck and fastened it.

JC went to the room off the altar to lend support to Tim and Molly joined the other bridesmaids in the cubicle in the vestry. Myra arrived and joined them, first frantic and then frozen, with nerves.

Finally the doors were closed and the mothers of the groom and then the bride were escorted to their seats. The wedding march began and they were moving down the aisle to the altar. Molly moved in the slow march with her head high and the touch of a smile on her face. Halfway down, she met JC's eyes and he smiled, if sadly, and held her gaze until she reached the altar.

She heard all the vows and produced the ring at the right time, but is wasn't Myra and Tim that were saying them in her mind, but she and JC. She snapped out of her reverie when she felt one scalding tear run down her cheek. Quickly she wiped it away with the back of her free hand and she hoped that no one had noticed. The bride and groom kissed and the music started. She faced JC and the look on his face told her that he had noticed. She tried to smile, but it hurt the muscles in her face. She took the proffered arm and they moved down the aisle behind the happy couple.

It seemed to take forever for the photographs to be taken and the wedding party to be off to the reception. A small hall had been rented and a band hired. A local caterer had the tables all set and the guests were enjoying drinks while they waited for the wedding party to arrive. The receiving line formed and Molly went through the motions of greeting and kissing more people than she cared to count. At last they sat down and went through the toasts and finally the food was served. Molly's lack of a breakfast and the three glasses of champagne suddenly made her feel quite happy about the situation that had caused her some misery a while before.

She entered into the spirit of the festivities with gusto and when she went to the dance floor with JC, she closed her eyes and pretended that they were dancing together again on the little dance floor in the harbor. His arms tightened and he whispered, "A penny for your thoughts, Molly."

"I was thinking about the only other time we ever danced."

"That was quite an evening as I remember it."

"Mmhmm."

They danced several times during the course of the afternoon, and Molly found herself searching for him when she had another partner.

The cake was cut and the bouquet thrown, Myra making sure Molly would catch it. At last the happy couple departed and the guests began to leave. This was Christmas Eve and most of them had lots to do to get ready for the holiday.

Molly's mother found her and said that they were leaving and asked if Molly would be riding with them. She was about to say yes when she spotted JC across the room, looking at her with questioning eyes.

"No, Mom. I have some things to tend to and I'll be home later. Don't wait for supper. I'm not sure how long I'll be."

She made her way across to him and he took her arm and led her to the coatroom. He placed her coat about her shoulders and they went out into the dusk of late afternoon. It was cold in the car and Molly shivered, hoping that it would not be long before the heater started to work.

"I'm sorry, Molly. I should have thought to warm up the car beforehand."

"It's all right." I drank enough so that I need some fresh, cold air to revive me."

"It was a nice wedding."

"Yes, it was. I really enjoyed myself at the reception."

"Are you ready to keep that promise?"

Molly nodded. "Yes, if now is when you want it to be."

"It is."

They drove through the dusk and Molly looked at all the Christmas decorations that made even shabby houses look festive. There had always been something magic about Christmas Eve that the day itself never quite measured up to. There was always the hope that, just maybe, that really special gift would be under the tree in the morning when you woke up.

"Where are we going, JC?"

"We are going to a place I know that will be quiet and where we are not going to meet anybody we know."

"Is it very far?"

"Not very. We will be there in a half hour or so."

Molly knew that they had entered Vermont when they crossed the Connecticut River, and she really didn't care how far they went because the further they went, the longer she would be with him. There was no one else she would rather be with on this Christmas Eve.

They left the highway and drove onto a narrow road that was piled high with snow on either side.

"Is this place yours, JC?"

"No, it belonged to Jeff and when he died, it went to Joan."

Molly sat up straighter and her relaxed feelings disappeared, replaced with a sudden feeling of betrayal. JC noted her reaction and said, "I think you will understand why I brought you here when you hear what I have to say and show you some things. It won't take long and then we can leave if you want."

The cottage was small and almost lost among the drifts. A path had been shoveled to the door and JC insisted on carrying Molly so she wouldn't wet her feet in the dainty satin shoes she wore. He turned on the light and went to the fireplace where the paper and kindling were laid for a fire. He struck a match and pulled her close to the flames. When the warmth began to penetrate the room, they sat on the couch in front of the fire and began to talk.

"When I told you that I loved you and wanted to marry you, I meant it with all my heart. I called Joan the next morning and told her about it and that I hoped she'd set a date for the service for Jeff. She became hysterical and said that I was betraying my brother and she would be no party to it. I didn't understand what she meant, but agreed to see her later that day. She told me that she had promised Jeff that she would take the honeymoon that they were planning and then that she would return and start a new life. He said that he hoped she could find that life with me. I was shocked. I always thought of Joan as a sister as she and Jeff were dating while I was in college and he was still in high school. She carried on for a long time about her loyalty and mine and, when I left, I told her that I had some thinking to do. I talked with Grandmother for a long time and she told me that she thought that I should make my own decisions and not let Jeff reach beyond the grave, so to speak, and direct my life for years to come. I agreed with her and decided that Joan would have to face the fact that he was gone and we were both on our own now. She met my remarks with an anger and lack of understanding that frightened me. I feared that she would take her own life and I could not live with that on my conscience.

She made me promise that we would be marred and that I would try to love her the way that she loved me. I was torn between my love for you and the memory of my brother and the girl he loved so much. Joan brought me here one afternoon shortly after you left. She wanted us to spend a weekend away from everyone. Sufficient to say, it did not produce the results that she had hoped for, but during that time, when I was unable to sleep, I investigated Tim's retreat more fully. At first I was looking for something to read and then I became curious about the desk that was so deep, but had such shallow drawers. Come over here with me, Molly, and I'll show you what I mean."

Molly rose and followed him to the small roll top desk in the corner of the room. Producing a key, JC unlocked the top drawer and Molly noticed that, instead of being the depth that the front implied, it was several inches shallower. JC removed the contents, which seemed to be rather standard desk items, and reaching far back underneath it, he turned a catch that made the bottom of the drawer that was beneath the surface one drop open. Several papers and what looked like a school notebook dropped out. He bent and picked them up carefully.

"These were my ticket to freedom from Joan and a final

legacy from my brother that is more precious to me than anything else."

He laid the notebook and papers out to Molly. She looked at them for a moment and then shook her head. "I don't want to read them, JC. I have a feeling that your brother meant them for your eyes only."

"I don't think that he meant them for anyone else to see but himself. Essentially, he began to suspect that Joan was in love with me and not with him a few years ago. He wrote his feelings about her and how he had pleaded with her to marry him several times and she kept delaying it for one reason or another. Then he made other observations that led him to believe that he was right, like the fact that she rarely went on a trip unless I was included. At first, I rejected the thoughts that he had recorded, and felt wounded to think that he died thinking of me as a stumbling block in the marriage he never had before he died. But his suspicions made me more alert to Joan's behavior, and I finally confronted her with the information that I had found. By that time, I guess she knew the futility of her scheme and she broke down and admitted that she had intended to tell Jeff on that trip that this was the end of their engagement and when he was killed, she felt a strong guilt, even though she had not told him yet. She needed time to deal with that, and also to keep a strong bond with me and Grandmother, so she came up with the story of the promise she had made to him. She was unwilling to make the final gesture of the service until she felt she had me safely engaged to her. She did not plan on you coming along and usurping the place that she had planned would be hers."

"It must have been terrible for you, JC."

"It was very difficult for both of us, but I think that she has gotten herself together now. Her family owns a home in Florida and she went there early this winter to stay for a while and decide what she would do next."

Molly looked up at him with tears in her eyes. "Oh, JC, you've suffered so much. And I haven't helped at all."

He pulled her into his arms. "I never gave up, Molly. I kept track of you and knew that the time would have to be right to approach you again." You have a lot of pride and I had to wait until some of the wounds had time to heal."

"When you sent me your mother's necklace, I knew that you

loved me. That kept me going, I think."

They kissed, like two people finding water after crossing a long, hot desert and, when he raised his head, he spoke softly, "Do you want to stay here or go home?"

"Take me home, please."

They both knew that she meant the home where her heart was.

Christmas morning, he carried her down the stairs wearing the red dress and when Mrs. Stark opened her bedroom door to their knock, he said, "Here she is Grandmother. Merry Christmas."

Martha F. Swain

ABOUT THE AUTHOR

Martha F. Swain is a retired school teacher born, raised and continuing to live in rural New Hampshire. I believe there are literally thousands of (now) adults who owe their ability to read at better than a 4th grade level and their knowledge of US State capitals to her teaching efforts. More importantly though, she taught by example the importance of practicality and common sense, with a consistency that would make any New Englander proud. She is also a sports fan of no small measure and knows more about professional football in general and the Green Bay Packers in particular than the vast majority of those who get paid to do so on television. Like all rational people north of the Connecticut border, she is also a devout Red Sox fan. I'm also going to speculate that, like many mothers, she may not fully realize the depth of love, respect and appreciation that her children have for her.

Made in the USA
Columbia, SC
11 November 2022